Mama, I'm Hungry!

A practical guide to child nutrition

By

Juhi Aggarwal

M.Sc. (Food & Nutrition)

UNICORN BOOKS

Publisher
UNICORN BOOKS
F-2/16, Ansari Road, Daryaganj, New Delhi-110002
☎ 011-23275434, 23262683, 23250704 • *Fax:* 011-23257790
E-mail: info@unicornbooks.in • *Website:* www.unicornbooks.in

Branch : Mumbai
23-25, Zaoba Wadi, Thakurdwar, Mumbai-401002
☎ 022-22010941, 022-22053387
E-mail: rapidex@bom5.vsnl.net.in

Showroom :
★ **PM Publications,** New Delhi
- 10-B, Netaji Subhash Marg, Daryaganj
  New Delhi-110002
- 6686, Khari Baoli, Delhi-110006

ISBN 978-81-7806-071-2
Mama, I'm Hungry!

Edition: 2014

Printed at : Param Offsetters, Okhla, New Delhi-110020

Dedication

This book is dedicated to my father-in-law, who was the epitome of simple living and high thinking.

Preface

One of the most challenging tasks faced by a young mother today is feeding her baby. What, how and when to feed her adorable infant are questions that assume prime importance. She realises that good nutrition is inseparably linked to good health. This book attempts to answer all these questions in a simplified and practical way.

The slow transition of the infant's diet from mother's milk to a liquid diet, from liquids to semi-solids, from semi-solids to soft diets and on to normal family meals is traced with meticulous care. Precautions and points to be kept in mind while feeding the young ones are emphasised repeatedly.

The recipes chosen for infants have been given special thought. First and foremost, they are most suitable for the intended age group, being nutritious and wholesome. At the same time, they are easy to prepare, made from readily available ingredients and economical too. Alternatives and options are given at the end of each recipe.

The basic principles of nutrition are relatively simple. A wide variety of food is available to the homemaker nowadays. Introducing food to the young ones with a smile and an open mind can lead to the development of lifelong healthy food habits.

So all you young mothers, fathers, caretakers, grandmothers, and grandfathers, get ready to cook a suitable meal for 'the apple of your eye'. Watch them clean their bowls, plates and tiffins with joy. I can visualise the satisfaction you will experience.

I am grateful to my husband, who has taught me to enjoy the simple things in life. I thank my two children, who were willing guinea pigs in my culinary experiments and provided constructive criticism!

Thanks also to Dr Ashok Gupta, who remains my guiding spirit and inspirational force.

Happy mealtimes!

—Juhi Aggarwal

Contents

Foods and Nutrition

While you can't recall what you did with your newborn all day, somehow it took every minute of your time.

The agony and ecstasy of childbirth is finally over. The parents are holding the most attractive bundle of joy in their hands. They aren't tired of examining the soft skin, the exquisite face and the tiny fists. At the same time, a feeling of apprehension shoots through them, as they are now responsible for an individual who is solely dependent on them for the fulfilment of his needs.

At this time the parents may be flooded with advice from relatives, neighbours, well-wishers and friends on how to bring up the child and what to feed him or her. This information may be correct, inaccurate, unfounded or outdated. It is important to learn to distinguish between food facts and misconceptions, nutrition folklore and correct scientific information. The media also keeps presenting the result of scientific studies. The reports are often contradictory and may leave the parents more confused than ever.

The basic principles of nutrition are simple. Nature has provided us with a wide variety of simple, nutritious food. It is up to the parents to give the child the widest options of foods leading to the development of lifelong healthy eating habits.

Simple Nutritional Facts

Before planning meals for her family, a young mother or caretaker should know some basic nutritional facts.

Food contains certain organic substances called nutrients. Our body requires six basic nutrients:

❖ Carbohydrates ❖ Proteins ❖ Fat ❖ Vitamins ❖ Minerals ❖ Water

Dietary fibre is also essential for the body. Different nutrients have different functions in the body. To function efficiently the human body needs energy, protein, a small amount of fat, 13 vitamins and at least 24 minerals. All these are required in small quantities but the amount of each is critical. Different foodstuffs are grouped into three broad categories on the basis of nutrients contained in them and their function. The three groups are shown in the chart below.

Food Group	Major Nutrient	Food Rich in the Nutrient
1. Energy-giving	Carbohydrates	* Cereals like wheat, rice, maize, jowar, bajra * Starches like potato, arbi, sweet potato * Fats like ghee, oil and butter * Sugars like table sugar, gur (jaggery), honey
2. Bodybuilding	Proteins	* Milk and its products like curd and paneer * Egg, meat, fish, chicken * Pulses like dals, gram, soyabean, peas, beans
3. Protective minerals and vitamins		* Green leafy vegetables like spinach, cabbage, methi, bathua, etc. * Other vegetables like pumpkin and carrots * Fruits like apples, oranges, papaya, etc.

Energy-giving Foods

We need energy to move parts of our body, to make substances inside the body and also for certain other bodily functions.

Bodybuilding Foods

Food provides energy for growth. Wear and tear of cells keeps occurring in the body all the time, so it needs to build new cells and repair damaged parts.

Protective Foods

Vitamins and minerals are required for most bodily functions. They protect the body against many deficiency diseases.

Simplified functions of various important vitamins and their sources are given below:

Vitamin	Function	Source
Vitamin A (Retinol)	Essential for normal growth of bones, teeth. Needed for good vision, healthy skin and tissue repair.	Milk, curd, cheese, green leafy vegetables, tomato, pumpkin, carrot, papaya, orange, mango, apricots, fish liver oil.
Vitamin B_1 (Thiamine)	Regulates metabolism, appetite, digestion. Needed for normal functioning of brain, heart and nervous system.	Milk, cheese, curd, meat, egg, yeast, wheat, nuts, peas, soyabean, legumes, dark green leafy vegetables.
Vitamin B_2 (Riboflavin)	Regulates metabolism.	Milk, meat, egg, germinated pulses, beans, yeast, green leafy vegetables.
Vitamin B_{10} (Folic acid)	Required for formation of red blood cells.	Green leafy vegetables, sprouted pulses, meat, fish, egg.
Vitamin B_{12} (Cyanocobalamin)	Essential for normal blood formation.	Meat, liver, fish, egg, milk.

Vitamin	Function	Source
Vitamin C (Ascorbic acid)	Required in the formation of all body tissues, e.g., bones, teeth, gums, protection against disease and healing of wounds.	Citrus fruits like orange, lemon, grapefruit, melons and in tomato, amla. Green leafy vegetables, cabbage, sprouted pulses.
Vitamin D (Calciferol)	Needed for proper bone and teeth formation. Helps in metabolism of calcium and phosphorus.	Sun rays, milk, butter, cheese.
Vitamin E (Tocopherol)	Needed for normal reproductory function.	Wheat, whole grain cereals, green leafy vegetables, alfalfa, milk, soyabean.

Some of the important minerals, their functions and their sources are summarised below:

Mineral	Function	Source
Calcium and phosphorus	Needed for hardening of bones and teeth. Needed for muscles and nerves.	Milk, cheese, egg, fish, green leafy vegetables, cereals, nuts.
Iron	Needed for formation of red blood cells and energy metabolism.	Liver, kidney, egg yolk, whole grain cereals, green leafy vegetables, jaggery, raisins, dates.
Iodine	Necessary for the formation of a hormone regulating body functions.	Fish, seafood, green leafy vegetables, iodised common salt.

It is important that your child has a nutritionally balanced diet. A 'balanced diet' denotes *eating the right food in the right amounts.* It is equally important, and perhaps more relevant today than ever before, that the right food in the right amounts should be taken *at the right time.* The nutrition pyramid is a simplified visual aid which tells you what to eat and in what amounts.

To follow the pyramid, we start at the bottom. The child should be given plenty of cereals (3–4 servings), which provide energy. The next part of the pyramid shows fruits and vegetables. These contain vitamins and minerals, which are extremely good for the skin, eyes and gums. These should be consumed in good amounts. The next rung of the pyramid has milk (1–3 servings) and milk products. These are important bodybuilding substances. Give two servings per day. Non-vegetarians can be given meat, fish and eggs in moderation (1–2 servings). The last level of the pyramid comprises fats and sugars. These are present in fried foods and sweets and should be consumed in moderation.

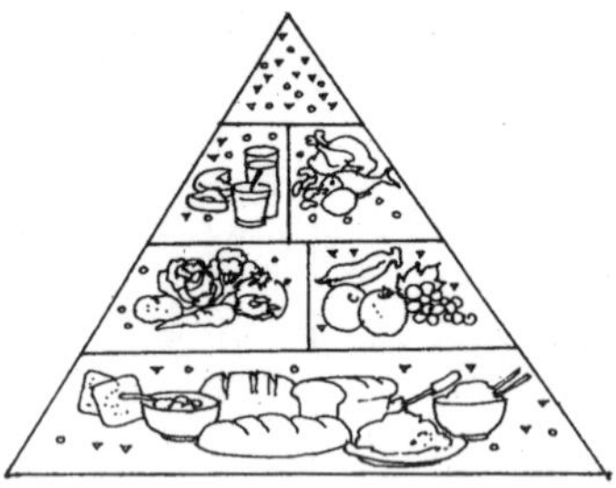

Let us look at the size of the serving in each food group.

Size of Serving in Food Pyramid

Food Group	One Serving
1. Bread, rice, wheat, other cereals, pasta	1 slice of bread or 1 *katori* cooked rice, pasta or one small chapatti.
2. Vegetables	1 *katori* of chopped, cooked vegetables.
3. Fruit	1 piece of fruit or three-fourths of a cup of juice or one-fourths of a *katori* of dried fruit.
4. Milk, cheese, curd	1 cup milk, 1 *katori* curd or 40 gm paneer.
5. Meat, egg, poultry, pulses	50 gm meat or 1 egg, 1 *katori* cooked pulses.

Latest Trends

New research has modified the food pyramid. They suggest that whole grain cereals should be consumed at most meals along with small amounts of vegetable oils. Vegetables should be consumed in abundance while servings of fruit should be limited to two or three. Nuts and legumes should be eaten in moderation as they help you feel full longer. Fish, poultry and eggs should be limited. Milk and its products are recommended. Red meat and butter should be eaten sparingly. White rice, bread, potatoes, pastas, and sweets should also be consumed in low amounts.

Nutrition in Infancy and Early Childhood

The importance of good nutrition for health can never be over-emphasised. While good nutrition is important throughout life, it is particularly essential from birth to early childhood. A nutritious diet along with tender loving care will make the baby grow into a physically and psychologically healthy adult and realise his full genetic potential.

There are millions of chemical reactions taking place in the human body. These help in sustaining life and growth. All these are dependent upon the nutritional status of an individual. Good, wholesome food allows the brain, bones and other organs to achieve full development. Studies also show that the development of personality patterns begins at birth and is closely related to feeding habits. Therefore, a mother's concern about good food for her little one is fully justified.

Foods for Different Organs

Although no single food can be said to benefit a specific organ, yet, studies indicate that consumption of some foods benefits certain organs more. Why not try and see whether you can make your child more intelligent and more athletic? The following organs are said to benefit from:

Brain: Carrots, broccoli, almonds, fish, leafy vegetables, strawberries, grapes, red cabbage, plums, olive oil, and sunflower oil.

Eyes: Citrus fruits, yellow fruits, carrots, pumpkin, tomatoes, papaya, guava, green leafy vegetables.

Lungs: Mangoes, carrots, spinach, capsicum, red bell peppers, tomatoes.

Heart: Fruits, vegetables, fish, low fat foods, whole grains, pulses, lean meats.

Bones: Milk and milk products, almonds, sesame or sunflower seeds, dark green leafy vegetables.

Skin: All yellow fruits and vegetables.

Intestines: High-fibre foods like whole grains, germinated pulses, fruits and vegetables.

Why Babies Need More Food

With advancing years, the nutritional requirements of an individual keep changing. On the basis of unit body weight the infant or a young child needs greater amounts of energy compared to an adult. Adults require energy for daily activities and the repair of worn-out tissues. Children need extra nourishment for rapid growth. Besides, children are hyperactive and need extra energy for all activities.

Nutritional Needs of Indian Infants

The Indian Council of Medical Research (ICMR) has recommended certain dietary requirements for Indian children. Let us look at the major nutrients required by infants.

Particulars	Body wt./ kg.	Energy calories /kg. body wt.	Proteins /gm body wt.	Vit. A ug	Vit. C mg	Calcium mg	Iron mg
0–6 months	5.4	108/kg	2.05/kg	350	25	500	Not given
6–12 months	8.6	98/kg	1.65/kg				

Energy

There is extraordinary growth in the infant's first year. So, the energy needs of the infant are high in terms of body weight. Till the first five months of an infant's life these needs are met by breast milk.

Proteins

There is rapid growth of bones, blood and tissues at this stage. The protein requirements are almost 2 gm/kg body weight.

Fats

At infancy the gastrointestinal tract of the baby has not matured sufficiently to digest and absorb fat. It is capable of digesting the fat in mother's milk. If other milk is given, it should be diluted.

Vitamins

The infant's requirements of vitamins are met by milk till it is 4 months old. If infants are kept indoors all the time, supplementation of vitamin D may be required. Breast milk contains adequate vitamins, although the milk of other animals lacks vitamin C. Supplementation of diet with juices and soups is recommended after 4–5 months.

Minerals

The infant has adequate stores of iron to last it for four months. Thereafter weaning foods rich in iron should be started. Calcium needs are met by milk.

Feeding the Newborn

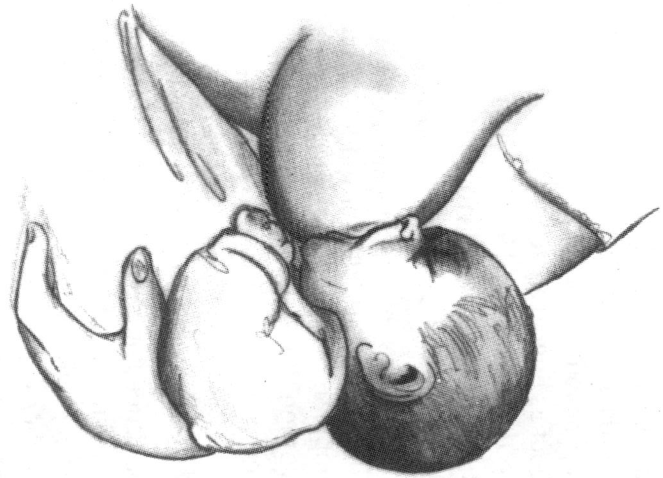

> *Morning routines with a toddler are anything but routine.*

The newborn learns to communicate his need for food by crying. After being led to the nipple by the mother for the first few days, he learns to seek, grasp and suck the nipple himself. The baby also learns to coordinate sucking, swallowing and breathing. He can digest and absorb nutrients required for growth and development. Doctors nowadays advise exclusive breastfeeding for the infant up to five months. Human milk is the natural food for infants. It contains most nutrients required by the child in the correct proportions.

Indian scholars have compared mother's milk to *'amrit'*. The *Charaka Samhita,* written over two thousand years ago, emphasises the importance of breast milk for the child. Indian women have been following this tradition since time immemorial.

Advantages of Breastfeeding...

Breastfeeding is simple, safe and clean. It helps promote loving attachment or bonding between the mother and child and can be enjoyable for both. The child feels safe and protected in the mother's arms. Breast milk is of the right nutritional value and composition as required by the baby. Studies have shown that breast-fed babies are more intelligent, healthy and smart. They grow up to be emotionally secure and stable adults.

For the Baby

For the first couple of days before the milk comes in, the baby gets only a few drops of colostrum. This is a clear, yellowish secretion rich in proteins, vitamin A and antibodies. It is the perfect food designed by nature for the newborn. The act of sucking by the infant stimulates the breast to start secreting milk. Colostrum also helps in the development of enzymes in the digestive system of the newborn. The more a baby sucks, the more milk is produced.

It is seen that exclusively breast-fed infants have several immunological benefits and they suffer from fewer gastrointestinal upsets and respiratory infections. Lactoferrin and lysozyme present in mother's milk inhibit bacterial growth and help the digestive system mature.

Mother's milk reaches the baby at the right temperature and there are no problems regarding sanitation. It is germ-free and no preparations are required. It is recognised that some flavours ingested by the nursing mother pass into breast milk. Thus breast-fed infants adjust easily to new foods while weaning. Breastfeeding also saves a great deal of money, time and bother involved in bottle-feeding a child.

For the Mother

Breastfeeding helps the uterus contract and return to normal more quickly after childbirth. It also delays ovulation and suppresses menstruation. Breastfeeding has some contraceptive effects when women do it for extended periods. The chances of developing breast and ovarian cancer as well as osteoporosis are lesser in mothers who breastfeed their babies.

Indian Studies on Breastfeeding

- Indian studies show that the incidence of illness in purely breast-fed infants is four times per year against 144 times per year in artificially fed babies.
- Breast-fed infants get protection from rotavirus infection, a major cause of deadly diarrhoea.
- They have added protection against asthma.
- They have less chances of becoming overweight.
- They do not develop allergies easily.
- They are more communicative and stable.

When Not to Breastfeed

- The mother suffers from some chronic illness such as tuberculosis.
- The mother is carrying her next child.
- The mother has to return to employment.
- The newborn is unable to suck due to some deformity.

Technique of Breastfeeding

The baby is given the first feed about 8–12 hours after birth. The infant is nursed at each breast for about five minutes so that the nipples are stimulated to produce milk. Later the feeding frequency is increased to feed the infant every 3–4 hours. During the first few weeks these intervals may be irregular. Later a feeding rhythm is established. After the second month, discontinue the night feeding. If the baby craves for the nipple at night, a small quantity of boiled water that has been cooled may be given to him. It is important to feed the baby in a calm and relaxed atmosphere.

Duration of Breastfeeding

This is a matter of individual preference. Some mothers may still be breastfeeding their 1½-year-old child. After this period it is better to wean off to animal milk as the quantity of mother's milk decreases gradually.

Non-availability of Mother's Milk

If mother's milk is unavailable or insufficient, the infant must be fed artificially or top-fed. The most popular substitute for mother's milk is cow's milk. Reconstituted powder milk is also used extensively nowadays. Cow's milk must be modified to resemble mother's milk as closely as possible. Milk powders have to be reconstituted with an appropriate amount of water to make the required amount of feed.

Most mothers breastfeed successfully as nature intended them to. However, certain circumstances may force you to opt for bottle-feeding.

Bottle-feeding

This is the common alternative to breastfeeding. Sometimes, additional bottle feeds may be given along with mother's milk if the milk supply is inadequate. Working mothers who are breastfeeding their children may resort to bottle-feeding when they are at work. Also, if the breastfeeding pattern is well established and the mother is absent during feeding time, she can induce secretion of breast milk in advance and have someone give it by bottle later.

Bottle-feeding Equipment

Such equipment consists of four to five good quality milk bottles with wide necks, silicone nipples, a bottle-cleaning brush, tongs, a sterile saucepan and a large saucepan to sterilise the bottles.

Preparation for Bottle-feeding

Take some cold water in the large pan and put the clean bottles in it. Boil the bottles for ten minutes. Put the nipples in and boil for another two minutes. Remove them from water. Fix the nipple and the bottle cover. Prepare a warm (body temperature) milk feed from fresh milk or dry milk powder. Strain this with a clean sieve. Sugar may or may not be added to the milk. Put this in the milk bottle and feed.

After feeding, rinse the bottle thoroughly with warm water and detergent. Rinse again with cold water. Pay special attention to the nipples. Turn them inside out and clean well. Rub with salt if slimy.

Points to Note

Prepare powder milk according to the directions given on the tin. Use the spoon or measure provided in the box. Measure ingredients accurately. Use levelled spoon or heaped spoon as directed. Add pre-boiled, cooled water to the milk powder. Stir with clean spoon. Prepare milk in a quantity that is adequate for the child. Do not make excessive amounts of feed. Throw away any leftover milk. Clean the bottle at the earliest. Leftover milk in the bottle provides a breeding medium for germs.

Before feeding, check the milk flow and the temperature of the milk by putting a few drops on the inside of your wrist. It should just be warm. Put the bottle in the infant's mouth so that the baby can suck. The nipple should be full of milk so that the baby does not suck air. Hold the bottle firmly. Air bubbles should appear in the bottle as the infant sucks. If they do not, remove the nipple slightly from the mouth and reinsert.

Do not prop the bottle against a pillow or let the infant hold the bottle himself. (At six to seven months the infant can hold the bottle.) This can prove to be dangerous and the infant could choke.

Do not let the child sleep with the bottle in his mouth. This may lead to tooth decay at a later age. Also, as the child becomes more mobile and independent, he might want to carry the bottle along with him as he moves. The child may not actually be hungry but just feels reassured and safe when he carries the bottle around. Do not encourage this habit, as it is not hygienically sound. It is also not wise to try to force-feed the child.

A mother who bottle-feeds her child should establish close physical contact with him. She can touch, cuddle or talk to the baby. Babies like skin contact with the mother.

Omitting Bottle-feeding Altogether

The duration for which a mother feeds her baby depends on individual preferences and circumstances like the urgency of joining work. Feeding the baby for a period of six months is very desirable, up to a year excellent and up to 1½ years admirable. Studies have shown that after this period the quantity of mother's milk may start dwindling.

Specialists nowadays suggest that bottle-feeding may be omitted altogether. Some suggest a feeder cup from the age of six months, while others recommend that the child be fed with a cup and spoon. A feeder cup is a fine quality plastic cup with a lid and spout. The spout has tiny holes. These holes help reduce the mess to the minimum. The baby can be trained to drink from this cup. He can easily hold the cup by himself when he is about ten months old. This method is not easy and requires infinite patience on the part of the person feeding the child.

Bottle-feeding seems very easy and convenient as compared to feeding by cup, but when the child has to be weaned off the bottle, it may prove to be a big battle. The older a child grows, the more difficult it becomes to persuade him to give up the bottle. It is easier to suck fluids from a bottle than swallow them from a cup. Many babies may give up drinking milk altogether, if forced to give up the bottle. One has to be patient and flexible while dealing with this matter.

Burping the Baby

Many doctors insist that there is no such thing as wind, but most mothers feel that the baby is more comfortable if they burp him. The baby is held upright against the shoulder and his back is patted gently. This releases any air in the stomach. The chances of the feed coming back are also reduced. Do not move the child vigorously after a feed, otherwise he may just throw up the feed. Some babies take a little time to burp, so be patient. Sometimes a baby may not burp at all. There may be no air in his tummy, so do not worry. Most babies do bring out some milk after a feed, so this is not a matter of concern.

4 to 6-month-old Baby

It is best to introduce weaning or supplementary foods between the ages of four and six months. The baby can now swallow liquid foods. The mature digestive system is now capable of absorbing nutrients from food. So, the weaning process can start.

What is Weaning?

Weaning is a gradual process of introducing supplementary foods in the diet of an infant so that the child is completely taken off mother's milk. The weaning period is very significant from the nutritional point of view. Selection and introduction of appropriate supplementary food becomes very important so that the infant gets a nutritionally adequate diet. In simple words, giving new foods is simply educating the baby about tastes and textures.

How Does One Wean the Baby?

Weaning can commence when the baby is four to five months old. The mother can omit one milk feed and feed the supplementary food instead. Gradually, the baby is given small quantities of different supplementary foods more frequently and the frequency of milk feed is reduced. Generally, early morning and late night feeds are retained. If the baby is kept only on milk feeds even after it is 6–8 months old, it may develop some deficiencies.

Preparation of Weaning Foods

While preparing weaning foods for your little one, keep the following points in mind to ensure that the food prepared is hygienic and wholesome:

- Hands should be washed thoroughly before preparing such food.
- The work area should be scrupulously clean.
- Pots, pans, juicers or any other containers used should be clean and sterile. It is best to use a small saucepan (kept separately) for the baby.
- Water used in any preparation should be properly filtered.
- The person preparing the weaning food should not be suffering from ill health or infections such as cold, cough, diarrhoea, etc.
- It is better to introduce weaning foods by means of feeder cups or bowl and spoon, rather than the bottle.
- Premixes can be prepared beforehand and stored in airtight containers in a cool place. It is safe to prepare a premix that can last for a week.
- Commercial weaning foods should be stored as per directions written on the container or the bottle.

- A dry spoon should be used to remove the premix from the box.
- The manufacturing date printed on packets and containers of commercial preparations should be noted carefully. Old, expired foodstuff should be discarded immediately.
- If the child rejects the food, do not be disheartened. It takes babies time to develop new tastes. Try again after a small interval.
- Do not add any spices to the weaning food. These can cause irritation in the child's delicate digestive system.
- There is no need to add sweeteners to food. However, if the juice is too sour, a little table sugar can be added. Excessive sugary foods are habit-forming and the baby may reject other kinds of food if it develops a sweet tooth.
- Salt is an acquired taste. Infants do not have a preference for it. So, weaning foods may only be mildly flavoured with salt.
- Food should not contain excessive fat. Fried foods should be avoided for the infant. As the digestive system of the child matures, he can be given relatively easily digestible fats like butter or cream.
- Place very small quantities of the food in the child's mouth. Let him ingest it. Then give the next spoonful. Do not hurry.
- Weaning foods should always be well cooked and easily digestible.
- Weaning foods should always be freshly prepared. Any leftovers should be refrigerated. It is better that an adult consumes leftovers instead of giving them to the infant again.
- The weaning food should be nutritionally adequate, easy to prepare, and made from locally available ingredients.

Preparing the Baby for the Feed

Mealtimes should be a happy time. Both the baby being fed and the person feeding it should enjoy the experience. Do keep the following points in mind:

- It is essential to tie a bib or a tucker round the infant's soft neck. The baby's habit of throwing out food like a cannon ball is common.
- If your room is carpeted, it makes sense to spread a plastic tablecloth over the feeding area.
- The child should be wide-awake at the time of feeding.
- Do not force-feed the child. Remember all the food can be thrown out at one go.
- A child can usually sit with support by the time he receives his first weaning food. Make him sit in a high chair. Some mothers prefer to keep the young one in their laps.
- If juices are given in a bottle, the pore size of the nipple has to be adjusted. Keep separate nipples for milk and juices.
- Keep the food out of reach of the infant's arms and legs. Their small legs have an uncanny habit of upsetting the whole feed.
- While feeding the baby with a spoon, place the spoon on the centre of the tongue pressing it very slightly.

Introducing Weaning Foods

Remember that all infant food must be given under close adult supervision. This prevents choking hazards. Also keep the following points in mind while planning and feeding the baby weaning foods:

- Introduce only **one new food** at a time, for instance, soup or *suji kheer*. Let the child develop a liking for it. The next food can be given after a gap of about a week. By this slow method of introduction of foods, a food allergy or intolerance, if any, can be detected. Some of the foodstuffs a child may be allergic to are wheat, eggs, nuts, etc.

- Initially the **quantity of weaning food** given may just be one teaspoon to a tablespoon. Newly born babies have extrusion reflex and this makes them push out any food from the mouth. They gradually learn to swallow liquids. As the baby grows used to the food, the quantity can be increased.
- Start with **thin purees**, and then move on to thicker soups. Thin, semi-solid purees can lead to slightly thicker, lumpy but well-mashed food. This can be followed by well-chopped, softer food.
- The food given to the little one should be **thermally bland**, i.e. it should neither be too hot nor too cold. It can be at room temperature.
- All the food given initially should be **mechanically bland**, i.e. it should be strained and sieved and not contain any fibre, e.g., strings of beans or pips of fruits.

6 to 9-month-old Baby

By now the baby can perform a host of new activities. He is ready to eat more solid foods. These may be in the form of thicker purees and slightly lumpy food. Some parents find that the baby sleeps better at night if he is given solids as feed before bedtime.

This is also the time when teeth begin erupting. Teething is a source of great distress to infants. Chewing seems to help as the gums are exercised. It is good to give the baby a teether to subdue the urge to bite. This is the time to introduce finger foods to the baby.

Finger Foods

These foods can be held in the hand and chewed by the child. They become soft in the mouth when a baby gnaws on them. Some good finger foods are rusks, toasted bread and butter, biscuits, raw vegetables like carrot, cucumber, etc. and fruits such as apples, pears, etc. Caution has to be exercised while giving finger foods. A child may sometimes bite off a big piece and choke on it. Always give these foods under close supervision.

This is also the time to make the baby get used to the feeder cup. The earlier a baby adapts to a cup, the better it is.

Hand-to-eye coordination improves by this time and the baby may like to wave, dig, and carry food with a spoon, resulting in messy mealtimes.

10 to 12-month-old Child

The biggest achievement of the child at this time is speedy mobility. As babies near their first birthday they may be speedy and crafty crawlers or adept walkers. The baby can hold his or her own cup steady. They can manipulate small pieces of solids in their mouth by means of the thumb and forefinger. They can feed themselves with a spoon and bowl, though spilling a little. Infants also learn to move food from one side of the mouth to the other and mash it.

Good eating habits should be encouraged at this point. Parents should not let their own prejudices affect the child's meal patterns. They should make the child develop a taste for a wide variety of food. Never show your own dislike for a food while offering the same to a child. Children who are given limited foodstuffs in childhood have strong fixed likes and dislikes and tend to become fussy eaters later on.

By the time the baby is one year old, he is ready to share family meals. From the cradle he has now reached the table. The child can eat whatever has been prepared for adults, but his portions should be removed before adding any strong spices or flavouring. For example, separate half a *katori* of boiled dal before applying cumin-asafoetida (jeera-hing) *baghar* to it.

Modification of Family Meals

Let us now look at some family meals to see how they can be modified to suit the small child.

	Family Meal	Baby's Meal
Breakfast	Tea, paneer parantha, curd	Milk, less spicy parantha, plain curd
Mid-morning	Tea, biscuits	Fruit
Lunch	Arhar dal, boondi raita, ladies' fingers sabji, chapatti or rice, onion-tomato-cucumber salad	Dal without *baghar*, plain curd, less spicy sabji, soft chapatti or boiled rice, cucumber
Tea	Tea, sandwich	Milkshake, sandwich
Dinner	Potato-peas, vegetable, gajar methi, chapatti, carrot, halwa	Less spicy vegetables, soft, small chapatti, carrot halwa

Remember that the baby's food should be a simple, less spicy, less fatty version of the adult food. Some points to note:

- Mealtimes should be pleasant. Try to create a relaxed atmosphere so that the baby can enjoy its meal.
- Try to serve meals at the regular time, when the child is fully awake.
- Ask the child to wash his hands before eating food.
- A child may be seated on a high chair along with other family members at the dining table. The child feels happy on seeing all members sitting together. Alternatively, seat him on a low, baby chair and matching table.
- Avoid highly spiced and fatty foods, tea, coffee, or highly flavoured vegetables.
- Remove pips, peels and strings from fruits and vegetables.
- Do not give a child hard nuts, sweets, toffee, etc. or he may get choked.
- Children like simple dishes. They may prefer plain boiled rice and dal to biryani, or plain curd to *dahi bhalla*.
- Steaming, baking, sautéing, and boiling are good cooking methods to be used for the child.

- Food should look attractive and appetising.
- Try to increase the variety by providing more colours, texture and flavours to the food.
- Most children require snacks between meals. It is a good idea to give them fruit, fruit juices, dry fruits, or *channa-murmura* at snack time.

Weaning Foods

We have seen that feeding is done in three stages:

- Liquid supplements.
- Semi-solid supplements - sieved and mashed well.
- Solid supplements - chopped, lumpy.

Liquid supplements

Animal milk slowly substitutes mother's milk. This has to be diluted to suit the infant's needs. Infant milk powders can be reconstituted and given to the baby. Juices or thin soups can be given after 4–5 months. Fish liver oil or any other supplements suggested by the doctor can be given.

Semi-solid supplements

The first semi-solid food is a cereal or starch food like potato, which is well cooked and mashed. Homemade or commercial cereal preparations may be used. Boiled mashed vegetables, boiled egg yolk, mashed dals, stewed fruit pulp, and mashed banana are other good supplements. Finely minced, well-cooked meat or fish may be introduced later on.

Solid supplements

Soft, well-cooked, chopped and lumpy food can now be given to be baby. Vegetable, potato, boiled rice, dal, chapatti soaked in vegetables or dal can be digested by the baby. Once the child starts having cereals, he should be given boiled, cooled water at least 2–3 times everyday. The quantity of water should be increased in summers.

Homemade Vs. Commercial Weaning Foods

Both homemade and commercial weaning foods are safe and nutritious. However, commercial weaning foods are expensive, quite bland and have limited flavours. Homemade weaning foods are fresh, wholesome, inexpensive and prepared lovingly, according to the baby's need.

Fresh Vs. Premixed Weaning Foods

Many weaning foods have to be prepared fresh daily. Some foods can however be partially cooked and stored in airtight containers. They can be reconstituted with warm water or milk when required. These foods are called premixes. Most premixes are cereal-pulse combinations along with nuts, sugar or oil. Fruits or vegetables may be added to them before feeding.

Reconstitution of premixes

1. Take 2–3 tablespoons of premix in a bowl.
2. Mix well with pre-boiled warm water or milk.
3. Add more sugar, if required.

FOODS FOR TENDER TUMMIES

Getting your toddler into the tub can be as hard as getting him out.

As mentioned before, your child's digestive system will not be able to handle all foods at this tender age. Therefore, a special diet catering to his tender tummy is required.

Some items that may be relished by your child are given in the pages that follow:

Orange Juice

Ingredients

Orange/mausami/kinu	–	3
Table sugar or glucose	–	1 teaspoon

Method

1. Extract the juice of the citrus fruit in a citrus juicer.
2. Strain if necessary.
3. Add a teaspoon of sugar if the juice is sour. No need to add sugar if the fruit is sweet.

- Be careful that the seeds of the fruit are not crushed while extracting the juice, otherwise the juice may taste bitter. The juice is rich in vitamin C and A and should always be freshly prepared.

Suitability: *4 months onwards.*

Tomato Juice

Ingredients

Tomatoes	–	150 gm (3 medium ones)
Sugar	–	1 teaspoon

Method

1. Blanch the tomatoes in hot water.
2. Cool and blend in liquidiser.
3. Strain, add sugar and a pinch of salt.

- Tomatoes are a rich source of vitamin A and C. Feed juice with spoon and bowl or use a bottle.

Suitability: *4 months onwards.*

Nutritious Soup

Ingredients

Tomato	–	100 gm (1 big)
Pumpkin	–	25 gm (small piece)
Cabbage	–	25 gm (small piece)
Onion	–	25 gm (small piece)
Moong (*dhuli*)	–	10 gm (2 teaspoons)

Method

1. Wash and chop the vegetables.
2. Wash the moong dal.
3. Put all the ingredients in a cooker along with two teacups of water.
4. Add 1 teaspoon of sugar and a pinch of salt.
5. Pressure-cook for five minutes after the whistle.
6. Let it cool and blend in a mixie.
7. Sieve and serve.

- Rich in proteins and vitamin A.

Suitability: *5 months to 5 years.*

Enriched Tomato Soup

Ingredients

Tomato	–	100 gm (1 big)
Carrot	–	50 gm (1)

Spinach	-	25 gm (few leaves)
Potato	-	25 gm (half)

Method

1. Scrape and clean all the vegetables.
2. Put the vegetables in a cooker, along with two teacups of water.
3. Add a pinch of salt and sugar.
4. Pressure-cook for two minutes after the whistle.
5. Cool and blend in a mixie.
6. Sieve and feed.

- Rich in iron and vitamin A.

Suitability: *5 months to 5 years.*

Vegetable Medley

Ingredients

Carrot	-	50 gm (1 small)
Bottle gourd (ghiya)	-	50 gm (small piece)
Peas	-	50 gm (1/3 *katori*)
Cabbage	-	25 gm (small piece)

Method

1. Wash, scrape and clean all the vegetables.
2. Cut into pieces of medium size.
3. Steam the vegetables.
4. Mash well with a fork.
5. Add a pinch of salt and a touch of ground black pepper.
6. You can add a blob of butter.
7. Mix well and feed.

- You can use any seasonal vegetables like round gourd (tinda), beans (with strings well removed), cauliflower or pumpkin.

Suitability: *7 months to 1¼ year.*

Cool Curd–Potato Mix

Ingredients

Curd	–	75 gm (3/4 *katori*)
Boiled potato	–	30 gm (small piece)

Method

1. Grate the boiled potato and then mash it well.
2. Add cool curd and mix well.
3. Add a dash of salt and feed.

- Infants like this taste. Make sure that the curd is fresh.

Suitability: *5 months to 1 year.*

Red Dalia

Ingredients

Germinated wheat dalia	–	15 gm (1 tablespoon)
Moong (dhuli) dal	–	15 gm (1 tablespoon)
Tomato	–	50 gm (1)
Tori	–	25 gm (small piece)
Oil	–	1 teaspoon

Method

1. Clean, scrape and grate the tori and tomato.
2. Add the oil in the cooker and roast dalia for a minute.
3. Add dal, tomato, tori and a pinch of salt.
4. Add 1½ teacups of water and cook for five minutes after the whistle.
5. Cool, blend well and feed.

- Add seasonal vegetables to salty dalia to get different flavours all the time.

Suitability: *8 months onwards.*

Evergreen Khichdi

Ingredients

Rice	–	15 gm (1 tablespoon)
Moong dal chilka	–	15 gm (1 tablespoon)
Spinach	–	15 gm (few leaves)
Bottle gourd (ghiya)	–	25 gm (small piece)
Oil	–	1 teaspoon

Method

1. Clean, wash and chop vegetables into small pieces.
2. Put the washed rice, dal, oil and vegetables into the cooker.
3. Add 1½ teacups water, a pinch of turmeric (haldi) and a pinch of salt.
4. Cook for 10 minutes after the whistle.
5. Cool, blend well and feed.

- Add any seasonal vegetables to khichdi. Cumin seeds *baghar* can be used for older children.

Suitability: *7 months onwards.*

Semolina Porridge

Ingredients

Milk	–	200 ml (1 glass)
Semolina (suji)	–	10 gm (2 teaspoons)
Carrot	–	25 gm (small piece)
Til	–	5 gm (1 teaspoon)
Sugar	–	10 gm (2 teaspoons)

Method

1. Dry roast semolina in a pan.
2. Roast the til separately and powder.
3. Wash, scrape and grate the carrot.

4. Cook carrot, milk and semolina together till slightly thick.
5. Add sugar and til and mix well.

- Semolina can be pre-roasted and stored in a tin for convenience.

Suitability: *7 months onwards.*

Stewed Apple

Ingredients

Apple	-	100 gm (1 big)
Sugar	-	1½ teaspoons

Method

1. Wash and peel the apple. Remove pips.
2. Cut into small pieces.
3. Put in a pan along with 1½ teaspoons of sugar and two teaspoons of water.
4. Cook for 3–4 minutes.
5. Mash, cool and feed.

- The same recipe can be used for stewed pear, apricot or pineapple.

Suitability: *5 months onwards.*

Fruity Custard

Ingredients

Milk	-	200 ml (1 glass)
Custard powder	-	1½ teaspoons
Sugar	-	1½ teaspoons
Banana	-	25 gm (1/3 normal size)
Chikoo	-	25 gm (small piece)

Method

1. Boil the milk with sugar.
2. Dissolve the custard powder in cold water.
3. Add to milk, stirring continuously. Cook for 2-3 minutes.
4. Peel, wash and mash banana and chikoo.
5. Cool custard, add mashed fruits and mix well.

- Mango, pear, papaya may be added instead of banana or chikoo.

Chirwa Milk

Ingredients

Milk	-	250 ml (1 glass)
Mota chirwa (flat dried rice)	-	15 gm (1 tablespoon)
Sugar	-	10 gm (2 teaspoons)

Method

1. Wash chirwa several times and soak in water for 10-15 minutes.
2. Boil milk with sugar.
3. Add to chirwa and let it swell.

- Use thicker chirwa made out of parboiled rice for this preparation.

Suji Besan Halwa

Ingredients

Suji	-	20 gm (4 teaspoons)
Besan	-	10 gm (2 teaspoons)
Oil	-	10 gm (2 teaspoons)
Sugar	-	10-15 gm (2-3 teaspoons)
Roasted groundnuts	-	5 gm (1 teaspoon)

Method

1. Grind the roasted groundnuts.
2. Sift besan and suji mix.
3. Put the besan-suji mixture in a pan, add some oil and roast over a slow fire.
4. When the mixture turns pink, add sugar and 3/4 *katori* water.
5. Stir till halwa consistency is obtained.
6. Cool, add groundnut powder and mix well.

- The combination of suji and besan gives good quality proteins.

Germinated Moong–Mash Raita

Ingredients

Curd	–	75 gm (1/2 *katori*)
Sprouted moong	–	10 gm (2 teaspoons)

Method

1. Steam sprouted moong for 2 minutes.
2. Mash well and add to smooth well-beaten curd.
3. Add a pinch of salt.

- Sprouted moong contains vitamins B and C along with proteins.

Germinated Wheat Dalia

Ingredients

Milk	–	250 ml (1 glass)
Germinated wheat dalia	–	15 gm (3 teaspoons)
Sugar	–	15 gm (3 teaspoons)
Roasted til	–	5 gm powdered (1 teaspoon)

Method

1. Dry roast the wheat dalia for two minutes.
2. Add milk and cook till dalia softens and blends with milk.
3. Add sugar and roasted til powder.

- Germinated wheat dalia is now available at most health food stores. Besides being more easily digestible, it contains vitamin E.

Fruit Yoghurt

Ingredients

Curd	–	100 gm (1 *katori*)
Sugar	–	5 gm (1 teaspoon)
Mango	–	25 gm (small piece)
Banana	–	25 gm (small piece)

Method

1. Hang curd in a muslin cloth for an hour till the excess water drains away.
2. Add sugar and beat slightly.
3. Add mashed mango and banana and blend well.

- Any seasonal fruits like pear or peach can be added to this.

Baby Poha

Ingredients

Chirwa flat (dried rice flakes)	–	20 gm (4 teaspoons)
Boiled potato	–	20 gm (small piece)
Boiled peas	–	20 gm (5–6 pods)
Lemon	–	½ piece
Oil	–	5 gm (1 teaspoon)

Method

1. Wash chirwa well.
2. Heat oil in a pan and add potatoes and peas.
3. Add chirwa, ½ tsp salt, a pinch of turmeric and mix well.
4. Add lemon and mix well.

- Mash potatoes and peas well to avoid choking hazard.

Suitability: *10 months onwards.*

Baby Upma

Ingredients

Suji (semolina)	-	25 gm (5 teaspoons)
Onion	-	25 gm
Oil	-	5 gm (1 teaspoon)
Lemon	-	½ piece

Method

1. Dry roast the suji in a pan.
2. Chop the onion very finely.
3. Heat oil, add onion and sauté for 2 minutes.
4. Add suji, 1 *katori* water and cook till halwa consistency is obtained.
5. Add lemon and feed.

- As the child grows older, seasonal vegetables can be added.

Suitability: *10 months onwards.*

Sprouted Kala Channa Khichdi

Ingredients

Sprouted black gram	-	15 gm (3 teaspoons)
Rice	-	20 gm (4 teaspoons)
Oil	-	5 gm (1 teaspoon)
Bottle gourd (ghiya)	-	25 gm (5 teaspoons)

Method

1. Heat oil in a cooker, add washed rice and black gram.
2. Add 2 *katoris* water, a pinch of turmeric and salt.
3. Grate ghiya and add to the dal-rice mixture.
4. Pressure-cook for ten minutes. Blend well.

- Soak black gram for 12 hours, remove and tie in wet muslin cloth for 24–36 hours till gram germinates. Germinated black gram contains vitamins B and C along with proteins.

Suitability: *10 months onwards.*

Cabbage Kheer

Ingredients

Milk	–	250 ml (1 glass)
Cabbage	–	50 gm (small piece)
Sugar	–	15 gm (3 teaspoons)
Cardamom (elaichi)	–	1 piece

Method

1. Grate cabbage and add to boiling milk.
2. Cook till cabbage and milk blend well.
3. Add powdered elaichi and sugar.

- Carrot or ghiya can be used instead of cabbage.

Suitability: *7 months onwards.*

Channa Murmura

Ingredients

Murmura (puffed dry rice)	–	50 gm (½ *katori*)
Roasted channa	–	25 gm (¼ *katori*)
Til	–	25 gm (5 teaspoons)
Sugar	–	10 gm (2 teaspoons)

Method

1. Roast murmura for 2–3 minutes and grind.
2. Remove husk of roasted channa and grind.
3. Roast til seeds and grind.
4. Grind sugar and mix well with other ingredients.
5. Store.

- Make sure that the roasted channa are of good quality and not coloured.

Suitability: *6 months onwards.*

Panjiri Premix

Ingredients

Atta (plain wheat flour)	–	50 gm (½ *katori*)
Besan	–	25 gm (¼ *katori*)
Groundnuts	–	15 gm (3 teaspoons)
Sugar	–	25 gm (5 teaspoons)

Method

1. Dry roast atta and besan for 5–10 minutes.
2. Dry roast groundnuts, remove, shell and powder.
3. Grind sugar and mix with other ingredients.
4. Store in an airtight box.

- Make sure you roast the dry ingredients on a low flame till a sweet fragrance is released.

Suitability: *7 months onwards.*

Soya Premix

Ingredients

Atta (wheat flour)	–	50 gm (½ *katori*)
Soyabean flour	–	25 gm (¼ *katori*)
Sugar	–	20 gm (4 teaspoons)

Method

1. Dry roast atta and soyabean flour on a low flame for 5–7 minutes.
2. Add powdered sugar and store.
3. Reconstitute this with warm milk at the time of serving.

- Soyabean flour is available in the market. Or you can get soyabeans ground. It is also a good practice to add 500 gm of soyabeans to every 10 kg of wheat to be consumed by the household.

Suitability: *7 months onwards.*

Rice Powder Premix

Ingredients

Rice powder tablespoons)	–	30 gm (2
Roasted channa powder	–	15 gm (1 tablespoon)
Soyabean flour	–	10 gm (2 teaspoons)
Skimmed milk powder	–	15 gm (1 tablespoon)
Sugar	–	20 gm (4 teaspoons)

Method

1. Roast all the dry ingredients separately.
2. Add skimmed milk and powdered sugar.
3. Store and reconstitute with warm water when required.

- Jaggery (gur) can be added instead of powdered sugar.

Suitability: 6 *months onwards.*

Toddlerhood Years
(1-3 Years)

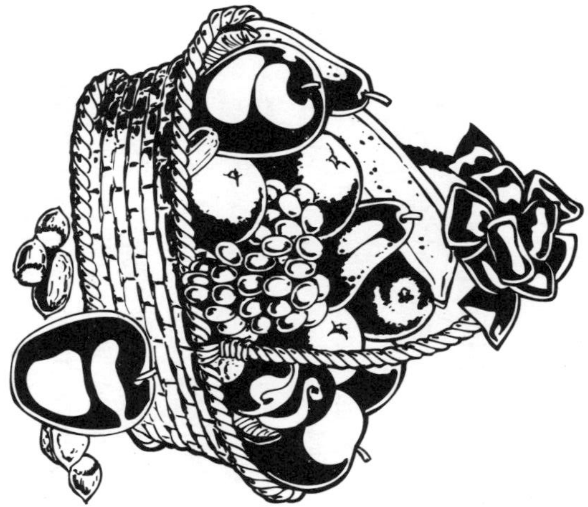

> *Toddlers are more likely to eat healthy food if they find it on the floor.*

'Always on the move' is a proper phrase to describe children in this age group. Curious, energetic, bubbly – it is hard to contain this young child. The child progresses through his first toddling steps to a full-scale sprint. The pitter-patter of tiny feet will now be heard throughout the house.

Prefers Simple Food

The food for a toddler is no different from an adult meal except that it consists of simpler, smaller portions. Toddlers prefer simple, uncomplicated meals. Thus they will like plain curd compared to raita, plain rice over pulao and plain dal rather than dal with vegetables.

Dislikes Vegetables

Children's aversion to vegetables is well known. However, vegetables are good sources of vitamins and minerals and should be incorporated in a child's diet. It is a good idea to wash, peel and hand slices of carrots, cucumber, kakri or even lettuce to the child on the move. Do not give raw peas as children might choke on them.

Too Much Milk Vs. Too Little Milk

Some mothers are always complaining that their little one does not eat anything. The problem may be that the child is getting too many milk feeds. He does not have an appetite for solid foods. Milk may fill the energy and protein requirement at this stage, but it does not have iron or vitamin C. By the time the child crosses one year of age, two to three milk feeds per day are enough.

Some children, on the other hand, give up milk altogether when forced to quit bottle-feeding. Milk is important for children, especially vegetarians. At these times, milk can be flavoured with chocolate additives or Rooh Afza. Milk shakes of mango, banana, chikoo and vanilla are liked universally. Milk can also be given as curd or paneer, or incorporated in kheer, kulfi, custard, ice creams etc.

Too Much of a Good Thing is Undesirable

A child's stomach is the size of a closed fist. It has a limited capacity. Some mothers feel that they should keep feeding the child all the 12 waking hours. Since health experts recommend fruit juices, they keep giving the child different juices at regular intervals. As the child's tummy is full of juice, he cannot take other solid foods, which are essential for growth. Besides, excessive fruit juice intake can lead to dental caries. And commercially packed fruit juices have high levels of food colours, preservatives and sugars. So, it is best to give one or two feeds of fresh home-extracted juice.

Foods Not Recommended

Children like mild-flavoured food. Therefore, an excess of over-pungent foods like garlic and radish should be omitted from their diet. Tea, coffee and other stimulants should also be avoided. Fried food is difficult to digest, so the quantity should be kept low. Excessive sweets, toffees and *mithai*'s should also be avoided. Some parents hand out sweets for every good deed the child does. Such bribery leads to increased expectations all the time. Sweet products are also called empty-calorie products, i.e., they may fulfil the child's energy requirements but are lacking in other nutrients.

Snack Time

The child is unable to eat large quantities of food at a single meal. Besides the normal four-meal pattern, the child can be given a mid-morning snack or a four o'clock snack. A snack does not mean a bag of potato chips or popcorn. Healthy snacks like fruit, fruit juices, channa-murmura, dry fruits, germinated chaat, etc. make good sense. The snacks should not diminish the appetite for the main meal.

Mealtimes Should be Regular

Meals should be given at a regular hour. It is up to the mother to decide whether it would be easier to feed the child half an hour before family meals or along with the other family members. Mealtimes should be pleasant. The child should not be forced to have meals. If the child wants to feed herself/himself, she/he should be allowed to do so. Hand-and-mouth coordination is not perfect at this age and there is bound to be spillage. It is a good idea to give the child smaller portions first. Subsequent helpings can be given to the child on demand. Also, give only half-full glasses of juice, water etc. to children because spilling of liquids on table-tops is common with them.

How to Serve

It is best to have a set of special dishes for the young one. These should be deep, as the child can use them with ease. Dishes with beautiful motifs of popular cartoon characters are now available in the market. A child can be quite possessive about his dish. Use small *katori*es and glasses for the child.

Mealtime is Not TV Time

Feeding time should not coincide with watching television. Some mothers find it easy to stuff food in a child's mouth while he or she is watching TV. The violence and drama normally shown on TV could easily divert the attention of children and thus encourage them to swallow food that should normally be chewed. I know of several children who refuse to eat food if they are not watching their favourite cartoon. Heaven help such parents if there is a power breakdown or the child is outdoors.

Fussy Eaters

If the child is a fussy eater, the caretaker can talk to him or tell him an interesting story to attract his attention. Do not run behind a child while feeding him. If this pattern is established, the mother may have to spend considerable time running after the child in order to feed it. Sometimes children use food as a powerful weapon to gain attention. So, if the child refuses food, don't worry. Simply offer it again after some time. A child will not remain hungry for too long.

Fall in Growth Rate

Keep in mind that the growth rate of toddlers is slower than that of infants. The average weight increase per year is now only about 2 kg. The increased requirement at this stage is due to increased physical activity.

Tips on Eating

- The child should be allowed to have only small bites. This allows for full mastication and saliva release. It keeps dental and digestive problems away.
- Do not give cold drinks along with food. Children gulp down drinks and little space is left in their stomach for food. Besides, these will hamper digestion.
- Water too should be preferably given after the meal is over. This ensures the child has his fill and there is proper digestion.

Pre-school Years
(3-5 Years)

There are no magic answers when it comes to raising your children – but there are many magic moments.

The pre-school years are characterised by outbursts of independence. The child may have irregular and erratic eating habits. Sometimes a child may refuse to have anything at all. The young one may also develop a single-food preference and demand the same food at all mealtimes, e.g., *aloo ka parantha* or French fries or noodles. This kind of food obstinacy is not healthy, as the child does not get nutritious food from the other food groups.

Easy-to-handle Food

Food given to a pre-schooler should be easy to handle. Children prefer finger foods that they can eat easily. For example, a child may not like to have a parantha with sabji. So, the parantha can be made into a roll with sabji inside. It can be wrapped in a foil and given to the child. He may relish it now, calling it *sabji wrap* or *chonga monga* (as our grandmothers called it). Alternatively, paranthas can be stuffed with gobi, muli, methi, bathua, etc. The child usually dislikes sticky, slippery food.

Breakfast and Tiffins

A pre-schooler may join a kindergarden or playschool at the age of three plus. Now he has become time-bound. Earlier he could sleep till late in the morning, but now he has to take a bath and be ready for school. Sometimes, breakfast suffers because of this routine. The child may miss breakfast altogether because he is getting late, or he may miss milk and just gulp down a few biscuits. Breakfast is an important meal and should ideally contribute one-fourth of the day's requirement. As the name implies, an individual *breaks* his *fast* when he takes this first meal of the day, almost 8–10 hours after dinner.

If the child misses his breakfast he may feel hungry before the lunch break. He may then act cranky and feel irritated or listless. This may lead to an unhealthy pattern of snacking on high-fat foods in between classes. Later on, the child may be tempted to have greasy burgers, patties, samosas, and bread pakoras from the school canteen.

Inadequate, Inappropriate Tiffins

Sometimes the tiffin given for school is inadequate. I have seen parents giving a few popcorns, chips, biscuits or sweets for lunch. Children of this age do not know what is good for them. It is up to the parents to decide what constitutes a good nourishing meal. If you ask the child what he would prefer for lunch, he may insist on a bag of chips, crackers, puffs or other junk food. You should decide the menu and let the child decide the quantity.

The child may become a fussy eater and bring back the lunch you gave him for school, uneaten. This may be due to many reasons, such as the anxiety of separation from the family, fear of the unknown, change in sleep and food patterns because of school etc. Interest has to be created in food. Also, the playschool supervisor can be asked to keep an eye on the child. A teacher's firm voice can sometimes work wonders.

Variety of Foods

Children, like adults, like variety in their food. The colour, flavour, shape, and texture of the food can be altered to increase food variety. Red paranthas (grated carrot mixed with dough), green parantha (spinach ground and mixed with atta), yellow rice (rice with turmeric), pink ice cream (ice cream with rose sherbet) may find favour with children. Children enjoy salty, sour, and sweet flavours. Lemon, mint, cumin seeds, etc. can be used to flavour food.

The food can be cut into different shapes to entice the child. Oranges can be segmented or cut into circular slices. Cucumber sticks or slices, tomato circles or wedges, grated carrot or sticks, radish flowers or sticks all add variety to the diet. A potato clown or tomato baskets attract a child's attention.

The food may be soft, crunchy or hard. Little ones like cornflakes, corn on the cob, germinated dals, pappad, dry fruits, etc. Chunks of fruits can be added to cornflakes and milk.

Meals are Social Events

Children at this stage are rapidly developing social and language skills. Meals are an important social event and a learning opportunity. The child learns to interact with friends at school and other relatives and friends at home. Group acceptance starts assuming importance. A child may not have a certain food item to eat at home but may share it with his friends at school.

It is a good idea to make the child join the school lunch programme, if the school has one. Some schools give a **fixed timetable** of lunches to be provided to the child by the parents. In this way, all children enjoy the same kind of food. For example:

Monday	:	Parantha and fruit
Tuesday	:	Poha
Wednesday	:	Sandwich
Thursday	:	Sprouts, salad
Friday	:	Idli or dosa
Saturday	:	Puri and sabji

It may be a bit taxing for parents to adhere to this schedule, but when they see cleaned-out lunch boxes they know their efforts have been amply rewarded.

Do not give messy, oily foodstuffs for tiffin. Many schools forbid children taking noodles, rice, chewing gums etc. to school.

Child Tantrums

Some children ask for snacks just before lunchtime or dinner. Do not bow to a child's wishes, even if the child whines or throws a tantrum. The child then gets used to having his own way. Nutritious snacks can be given in between meals but cakes, cookies, chocolates and sweets should not form the bulk of the child's diet.

Adults as Role Models

The child develops a liking for nutritious food only when all family members sit and share the same meals. A child cannot be expected to eat health food if the other family members eat junk food. Adults in the family have to set a good example. Once the child starts going to school, parents can talk about good eating habits. They can reinforce nutrition lessons taught in school.

What is Junk Food?

Foods with high calorie, fat, sugar and salt content and low protein, vitamin and mineral content are called *junk foods*. Since they only provide calories without contributing any significant amounts of other nutrients, they are also called *empty-calorie food*. Junk foods are generally low in fibre and have less satiety value.

Salted snack foods, candy, gum, desserts, French fries, burgers, pizzas, cakes, biscuits, fried snacks and carbonated beverages usually fall in this category. Junk foods are normally prepared from potato, maida, sugar, butter and oil. Salted snack foods have many artificial additives that are used to prolong the shelf life of food or enhance its colour, flavour and texture. Excess preservatives are detrimental to health.

Junk foods are supported by enormous advertising, which dwarfs any attempt to educate the child about healthy diet. Junk food manufacturers target children with free toys, cartoon characters, and gimmicky packaging to ensure that children pester their parents for the product advertised.

Generally, a good rule of thumb is to give children fresh, healthy food 90 per cent of the time and junk food only 10 per cent of the time.

- Studies show that children who drink colas in excess are fat, weak-boned, cavity-prone and addicted to caffeine. Chocolate is considered nutritious when had in small amounts. But when consumed in large amounts on a regular basis, it is unhealthy and fattening.

Making Junk Food Nutritious

There is no harm in going for pizzas, noodles and burgers once in a while. Remember to add plenty of vegetables as toppings. If the child removes chunks of vegetables from the noodles, you can try grating or mixing the vegetables. Soya chunks, sprouts, and salads can be added to burgers or sandwiches.

Who is a Healthy Child?

A chubby or plump child is not necessarily a healthy child. Some overzealous parents stuff their children with ice creams, cakes, biscuits, cold drinks etc. A fat infant may look adorable but a fat adolescent does not. It is not that carbohydrates and fats are restricted at this stage, but they should be given in moderation. A child need not be given a dessert or *mithai* after every meal. Remember an active and alert child is a healthy child.

Points to Ponder

To summarise, remember the following points:

- Include foodstuff from all food groups in your daily meals, e.g., whole grain cereals, pulses, fruits and vegetables, milk and milk products, eggs and meat. Vegetarians can have more of nuts, pulses and legumes.
- Use all methods of cooking, e.g., steaming, boiling, roasting, sautéing, shallow frying etc.
- The goodness of *dal-roti*-vegetable combination can never be over-emphasised.
- Food habits acquired at this stage may last a lifetime. Inculcate a wide variety of tastes in the child.
- A child's meals should be like family meals. If the whole family is having *palak paneer,* a mother should not prepare *jeera alu* specially for the child.
- Use vegetables and fruits that are in season. Out-of-season products are bland, juiceless, tasteless and expensive. At the same time, it means that they have been grown and stored using artificial means.

Is My Baby Growing Well?

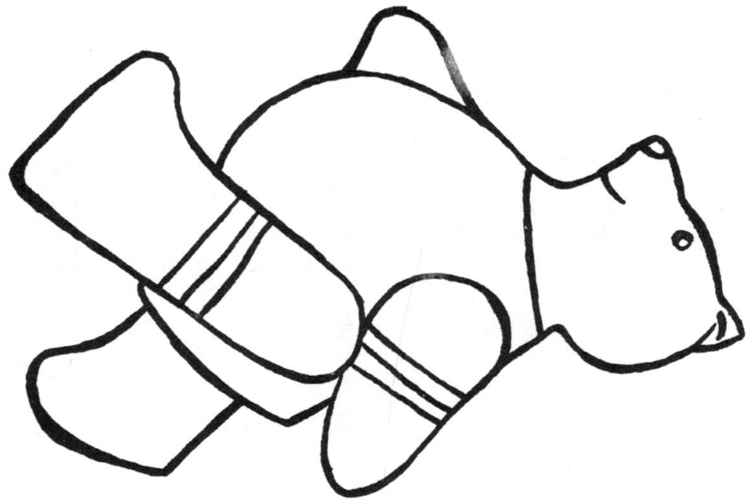

Once you have a second child, you realise that having the first one didn't make you an expert.

At some time or the other, young mothers are plagued by the doubt whether their baby is growing normally or not. Every infant is an individual and cannot be compared with others by any set standards.

However, several observations do show whether the baby is well nourished or not:

- There is steady gain in height and weight.
- The baby is happy, energetic and sleeps well.
- The baby has firm muscles and a moderate amount of baby fat.
- Teeth begin to erupt by six to seven months of age.

As you know, infancy is a period of rapid development. A child doubles his birth weight of 2.5–3 kg and reaches 6 kg in five to six months. He triples his birth weight by the time he is a year old. Similarly, the baby increases his birth length of 50–55 cm to 70–80 cm by his first birthday. To have a better idea of what to expect, you can check the table below.

Boys

Age	Weight (kg)	Height (cm)
Birth	3.3	50.5
3 months	6.0	61.1
6 months	7.8	67.8
9 months	9.2	72.3
1 year	10.2	76.1
2 years	12.3	85.6
3 years	14.6	94.9
4 years	16.7	102.9
5 years	18.7	109.9

Girls

Age	Weight (kg)	Height (cm)
3 months	5.4	60.2
6 months	7.2	66.6
9 months	8.6	71.1
1 year	9.5	75.0
2 years	11.8	84.5
3 years	14.1	93.9
4 years	16.0	101.6
5 years	17.7	108.4

Average Weight and Height Increments *(First Five years)*

Age	Weight Increment Per Week
0–3 months	200 gm
4–6 months	150 gm
7–9 months	100 gm
10–12 months	50–75 gm
1–5 years	2.0 kg per year

Age	Length Increment Per Week
1 year	25 cm
2 years	10–12 cm
3 years	7–9 cm
4 years	6–8 cm
5 years	6–8 cm

These are average Indian figures but the baby should be compared in relation to his own birth weight. It is a good idea to know what kind of activities to expect as the child grows. The physical and motor dexterity achieved at certain ages is also called the child's *milestones*. Check if your youngster has achieved them. Individual differences in babies do exist. A few months less or more does not make much difference.

Age	Activities to Expect
1st month	A baby sleeps for about 15 hours a day; can see and focus, hear sounds, lift its chin if placed on its tummy.
2nd month	Kicks at random, can pull arms together, lift chest if placed on its tummy; begins to gurgle and squeal with delight; sucks fists.
3rd month	Can hold a rattle, roll over, wriggle; uses legs and hands randomly; can recognise the mother or a person who attends to him.
4th month	Naps get shorter and the baby begins to reach. Studies own hands and feet.
5th month	Can sit with support; can transfer an object from one hand to another; can hold a spoon; can play with soft toys, blocks, etc.
6th month	Can sit without support; watches different kinds of movement; can sit independently on a high chair and handle a spoon (with very messy results); begins to recognise two or three family members.
7th month	Can hold a bottle or feeder cup; attempts to crawl; cuts his first tooth; constantly babbles sounds like ma-ma, da-da, na-na, etc.
8th month	Discriminates between family members and outsiders. Learns to drop things; gets better at crawling; can stand with support, cruise on furniture, drink from a cup and chew food.
9th month	Can stand independently, pull to a standing position from a sitting position and walk with support; can wave goodbye.
10th month	Can pick up small objects with thumb and finger; can sit and stand.
11th month	Learns to communicate using simple words. More teeth appear.
12th month	Can walk independently; can talk with simple two-word sentences.
18th month	Can crawl and climb stairs, or throw a ball; vocabulary increases.
2 years	Can run, climb up and down, play with food, toys, blocks and turn the pages of books.

Age	Activities to Expect
3 years	Can climb, jump, throw a ball, ride a tricycle, dress and undress and stand on one leg.
4-5 years	Can skip, jump, catch and throw independently.

Major Nutritional Requirements of Children *(1-5 Years)*

<table>
<tr><th>Age</th><th>Body wt/kg</th><th>Energy calories</th><th>Proteins gm</th><th>Vit. A ug</th><th>Vit. C mg</th><th>Calcium mg</th><th>Iron mg</th></tr>
<tr><td>1-3 yrs</td><td>12.2</td><td>1240</td><td>22</td><td rowspan="2">400</td><td rowspan="2">9</td><td rowspan="2">400</td><td>12</td></tr>
<tr><td>4-6 yrs</td><td>19.0</td><td>1690</td><td>30</td><td>18</td></tr>
</table>

ICMR figures

On reaching one year, the child's growth rate slows down in comparison to the infant's. The child graduates to an adult-style diet and requires a good quantity of proteins for growth and repair of worn-out tissues. All vitamins are required in good quantities for maintenance and prevention of disease. Calcium and phosphorus are required for good growth of bones and teeth, while iron is needed for increasing blood volume.

To meet these requirements, it is best to follow the portions suggested in the food pyramid. Note the following characteristics in a healthy child:

- Is alert, happy, active, sleeps well, and is not irritable or restless.
- Has normal weight in accordance with age and height.
- Erect posture.
- Smooth skin with healthy glow.
- Shining hair.
- Clear, bright eyes with no dark circles around them.
- Firm and well-developed muscles.
- A good appetite.
- Good attention span.

Food Allergies

> *Reading a story to your child every night is as good for you as it is for her.*

Your baby has just had his meals and a few hours later is afflicted by a runny nose and sneezing. Diarrhoea, vomiting or skin rashes could follow this. Could it be a reaction to some food? Perhaps or perhaps not... Only trained doctors could differentiate between food allergies and common childhood ailments.

Foods Commonly Associated with Allergies

Food allergies are most common in infants and young children. Eggs, milk and wheat are the most common culprits. Most food allergies are outgrown by the age of three, perhaps because of a maturing immune system. Fish, meats, nuts, mustard, tomato, soyabean, celery, chocolates and oranges are some other foods commonly associated with allergies.

Wheat is a staple in the diet of many Indians. In coeliac disease or gluten intolerance, gluten - a protein found in wheat, barley, rye and oats - destroys the small intestine's ability to absorb nutrients from food. Peanut allergy is one of the most prevalent and serious food allergies. To avoid milk in the case of lactose intolerant infants is a daunting task.

Food Allergy Vs. Food Intolerance

In allergies, the body's reaction is sudden and more pronounced. The reaction is usually delayed and subtler in intolerance. In allergies, a foreign body (allergen) triggers an immune system response producing antibodies called immunoglobulins. These in turn cause release of histamines, which lead to multiple symptoms.

The immune system is not involved in food intolerance. Intolerance or food sensitivity could be due to a variety of reasons like enzyme deficiency. In lactose intolerance, the body cells lack an enzyme called lactase and, therefore, the body is unable to digest milk sugar (lactose). Another reason could be a chemical such as caffeine. One person may feel jittery with just one cup of coffee, while another may have several cups with no symptoms whatsoever. If you suspect your child has some allergy or intolerance, visit an allergy specialist immediately.

Dietary Treatment

• *Elimination of the causative food*

If a food is identified positively, it should be eliminated from the diet. Then the symptoms of the allergy will slowly subside and not recur. If the food is an uncommon one, e.g. shellfish, it can be avoided easily, but it is difficult to avoid common foods like milk, eggs and wheat because they are also used widely in other preparations. For example:

- Milk gives us dairy products like cream, curd, paneer, whey.
- Wheat is used to make chapattis, dalia, maida and suji biscuits, bread, noodles, soups, gravies, etc.
- Eggs are used to prepare cakes, pudding, biscuits, dressings, etc.

It is necessary to read the labels carefully while buying packed or canned food from the market to weed out these allergens.

• *Substitution by alternative foods*

A child sensitive to cow's milk may not be sensitive to goat's milk. In such a case, goat's milk may be used as an alternative. Various preparations of soyabean milk and soyabean milk powder are now available in the market. Being rich in protein, they are a good substitute for children suffering from lactose intolerance. A child sensitive to wheat thrives well on a diet of rice, maize, oat or barley. Children sensitive to eggs can be given eggless cakes, puddings, biscuits, besan chillas, etc.

• *Change in the nature of allergen*

Sometimes a patient may be sensitive to raw milk or lightly cooked eggs, but can tolerate well-cooked eggs and boiled milk. This is due to the change in the quality of protein in milk or egg, when they are heated. Some patients may only be sensitive to egg white and not egg yolk. In this case, the egg yolk may be separated from the egg white and given to the patient.

- ***Desensitisation***

Sometimes very small quantities of allergen may be given by mouth or injected repeatedly to desensitise patients. This method has to be adopted only under close medical supervision.

- ***Effects of Age***

Patients tend to outgrow their sensitivity to food allergens. Seventy to eighty per cent children with milk intolerance will be able to tolerate milk by the age of four.

General Precautions

- If there is family history of food allergy, be very careful while introducing new foods in an infant's diet. Introduce only one food at a time and watch its effect.
- Avoid food that one is allergic to. Strict adherence to allergen-free diet is a must at all times.
- The family doctor should be aware of the allergy.
- Eliminating a food from the child's diet can prove to be very challenging, especially if it is milk or wheat. Find alternative foods that appeal to your child and will make up for the missing nutrient. For example, if milk has to be eliminated, find other rich sources of calcium, protein and vitamin D. If the diet has to be free from wheat, find rich sources of B complex vitamins, iron and fibre.

Substitute Foods

In the table that follows, you can check out the alternatives or substitutes for foods you have to avoid.

Actual Food	Replacement
Wheat flour Suji Maida	Rice flour, potato starch, broad beans flour or tapioca flour. Gram flour, besan or rice rava. Rice flour, potato starch, broad beans flour or tapioca flour.
Egg	Condensed milk, evaporated milk, curd or egg replacer (consists of starches and leavenings).
Milk Paneer	Soya milk, oat milk, or rice kanjee. Tofu (soyabean milk paneer).
Sugar	Honey, dates, fruit juices and artificial sweeteners.
Soyabean	Peanuts, peas, rajma, channa and germinated pulses.
Peanut/groundnut Peanut oil	Almonds, walnuts and cashew nuts. Corn oil, sunflower oil, mustard oil, safflower oil, olive oil and soyabean oil.

Special Recipes for Children with Wheat Allergy

Rice Flour Parantha

Ingredients

Rice flour - ½ *katori*

Oil - 2 teaspoons

The dough should be kneaded 5–10 minutes before the parantha is required, otherwise the dough turns very soft, moist and sticky and is very tricky to handle.

Method

1. Sift and knead the flour.
2. Make small balls and roll like regular paranthas.

3. Roast on tava on both sides.
4. Apply oil and fry on both sides.

Mixed Flour Chilla

Ingredients

Rice flour	–	1/3 *katori*
Maize flour	–	1/3 *katori*
Besan	–	1/3 *katori*
Onion	–	1
Cabbage	–	Small piece
Carrot	–	1
Salt	–	¾ teaspoon
Oil	–	1 tablespoon

Method

1. Sift all flours, mix together, add salt and make a batter.
2. Chop onion, cabbage and carrot finely and add to the batter.
3. Make small chillas on a non-stick tava using a little oil.

- Mixture of 2–3 flours always works better than one single flour.

Rice Flour Pancakes

Ingredients

Rice flour	–	1 *katori*
Curd	–	½ *katori*
Egg	–	1
Salt	–	½ teaspoon
Sugar	–	1 teaspoon
Soda	–	A pinch
Oil	–	1 tablespoon

Method

1. Mix all the ingredients together and beat well.
2. Prepare small pancakes on a non-stick frying pan.

- Mixture of 2–3 flours always works better than single flour.

Special Recipe for Children with Milk Intolerance

Soya Milk

Ingredients

Soyabean	–	20 gm
Jaggery or sugar	–	15 gm
Water	–	200 ml

Method

1. Soak soyabean overnight.
2. Remove the skin and grind to a paste.
3. Dilute with water and boil.
4. Add jaggery, sugar or honey.

- Soya paneer and tofu can be prepared from this soya milk, similar to normal paneer. To mask the strong taste of soyabean, flavours like vanilla and pineapple can be added to cold soyabean milk. Soyabean milk or soyabean powder is available in the market under many brand names, e.g., Sip-Soy, Soyal etc.

Food for Health

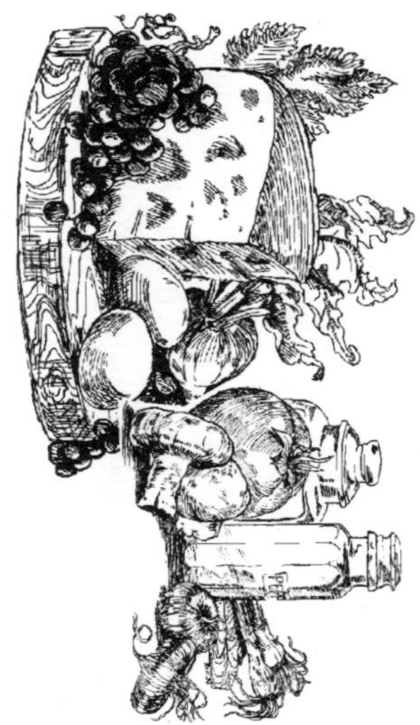

> *Children follow in your footsteps faster than they follow your advice.*

Just like healthy children, sick children need to eat. In fact, they need extra food and nutrients to make up for weight loss. If sick children do not get enough food, they lose weight and become malnourished. The saying that an empty stomach helps recover faster is outdated. Some children are finicky eaters and also suffer from a lack of appetite. Feeding such children becomes very tricky.

For infants of less than six months, continuation of breastfeeding is the best. The mother should increase the frequency of breastfeeding, as the infant might not be able to take a good amount of feed at one time, especially during night.

- Intervals between mealtimes should be reduced. Smaller and frequent meals are best.
- Nutritious snacks like lassi, fruit juices, biscuits and fruits should be given.
- More food should be given during the recovery period.
- Soft, bland diets of porridge and purees are best for the little ones.
- For children suffering from diarrhoea, use rice, curd, washed dals, banana, peeled apple, ghiya, and tori in the diet.

Malnutrition in Childhood

The food intake of a child may be inadequate, imbalanced or excess. This is termed malnutrition. Inadequate nutrition is more common in the lower income group while over-nutrition is seen mostly in higher income groups. Imbalanced nutrition can exist in all classes.

Inadequate Nutrition

Nutritional deficiency is called primary deficiency if there is inadequate intake of food. It is called secondary nutritional deficiency if the diet is adequate but there is a problem in digestion and absorption of nutrients.

How does a mother or caretaker recognise if her child is indeed malnourished? For this, she can be alert to the following signs:

- The child does not attend school regularly and has poor attendance.
- The child is very thin and fails to grow in height.
- The child is easily tired and remains listless, depressed, irritable, cannot concentrate for long and sleeps less.
- The skin looks pale, has patches, and wounds do not heal.
- The hair looks dull, lifeless, sparse and can easily be pulled out.
- The eyes burn and itch, and there is poor vision at night. The eyes may also be swollen or congested.
- The mouth may be swollen, lips may be extra red, and there may be cuts at the corners of the mouth. The child may suffer from an inflamed tongue and frequent boils in the mouth.
- The teeth may have caries and poor chewing strength. The gums may bleed.
- The child may have poor posture and show deformities of the bone.
- The child may have muscular weakness, flabby muscles and poor coordination.
- The neck gland thyroid may be enlarged. The child suffers from repeated cold and other infections.
- The child has a poor appetite, a potbelly and may suffer from frequent diarrhoea bouts.

In the initial stage of deficiency, the physical signs may be absent but biochemical changes slowly take place in the body. With further depletion, physical signs become more pronounced.

Some specific symptoms of common deficiency disease are enumerated below:

Lack of energy foods

- Weight is below average.
- Growth rate of the child slows down.
- He is an irritable, inactive and unhappy child.
- Disappearance of fat from the body.
- Wrinkled skin.

Lack of protein rich foods

- Fall in growth rate.
- Child is apathetic and irritable.
- Child may look plump due to water accumulation in the tissues.
- The child's face may look swollen.
- There is discolouration of hair, which may turn golden, brown or red.
- The skin may look patchy and peel off.

Lack of vitamin A

- Low vision at night.
- Patchy skin.
- Progressive degeneration of eyesight.

Lack of B-complex vitamins

- Poor appetite and irritability.
- Constipation.
- Sensitivity to bright light, burning and itching in eyes.
- Skin peeling off near nose and mouth.
- Pins and needles in feet.

Lack of vitamin C

- Sore, bleeding gums.
- Pinpoint red spots.
- Poor bone and teeth development.
- Slow healing of wounds.

Lack of vitamin D, calcium and phosphorus

- Soft, fragile bones.
- Delayed teeth eruption.
- Deformities of bones.

Lack of iron and folic acid

- Anaemia.

At one end of the spectrum while we see undernourishment, at the other end the problem is excessive nutrition. One of the most common examples of over-nutrition is obesity.

Small Babies, Big Problems

Although every mother wants her child to be healthy, do remember that chubby is not always healthy. An active and alert infant who reaches his milestones on time is healthy. A fat, nine-month-old infant may be unable to stand because his legs cannot support his body weight. Obesity in children is assuming great magnitude abroad and is slowly creeping into affluent families in India also. A study of Delhi schoolchildren showed that every 15th child is obese.

Who is Obese?

An individual whose body weight is more than 20% the normal weight for his age and height is said to be obese. For example, the average weight for a five-year-old Indian child is 17–18 kg. A child who weighs more than 22 kg would be termed obese.

What Causes Obesity?

When the intake of energy is more than the body's requirement, fat starts accumulating in the body. One of the major reasons for this is:

Faulty Food Habits

- Excessive desserts, butter, cream, and *mithais*.
- Excessive snacking on junk foods such as pizzas, burgers and French fries.
- Eating snacks like chips, popcorn, munchies or biscuits, while watching TV.

Faulty food habits are further compounded with little or no exercise. Studies also show that the possibility of a child with normal weight parents becoming obese is eight to ten per cent. If one of the parents is obese, the possibility increases to 40%. However, if both the parents are obese, the possibility climbs to 80%.

Hazards of Obesity

Fat infants become fat adolescents and later on fat adults. They are more susceptible to hypertension, coronary heart disease, diabetes, arthritis and a host of other ailments.

Increase in Fat Cells

People may love a fat infant, but fat adolescents become a source of worry. When a child is overfed in infancy, the fat starts getting stored in the adipose tissue. The quantity of these cells increase normally till the age of one. After this age, the cell numbers do not increase but the size of the cells increases. In fat infants, the number of fat cells also keeps increasing. Thus a fat child has more chances of becoming a fat adult. If a person starts dieting at a later age, the cell number cannot decrease. Also, the chances of regaining the lost weight are very high.

Prevention of Childhood Obesity

The main point to be emphasised here is the proper selection of foodstuffs. Carbohydrate rich foods like rice, potato, noodles, banana, biscuits and oily foods are to be given in moderation. The child should be made to develop a taste for paneer, pulses, eggs, fruits, vegetables, juices, soups etc.

The family's feeding habits should also be healthy. In some families, consuming paranthas for dinner daily is a must. However, phulkas at night are more suitable and lighter on the stomach. Similarly, all meals do not have to be followed with a dessert. Sometimes shelves at homes are stacked high with chips, namkeens, fried groundnuts, etc. It is difficult for a child to resist the temptation of snacking. Bribing a child with chocolates, sweets, pastries and ice creams is also common. It has become difficult for children to imagine watching a movie without a bagful of buttered popcorn and cold drinks. We Indians are also very fond of consuming *mithais,* chocolates etc. when we go visiting relatives or friends. And when guests come over, we love to force them to have more and more helpings of puris, sweets and other oil rich foods.

All the wrong eating habits contribute largely to the problem of obesity.

Sample Menu for an 8-month-old Child

Time	Monday	Tuesday
6.00 a.m.	Milk - 1 small glass	Milk - 1 small glass
9.00 a.m.	Suji kheer - ½ *katori*	Channa murmura premix - ½ *katori*
11.00 a.m.	Orange juice - ½ small glass	Tomato juice - ½ glass
1.00 p.m.	Nutritious khichri - ½ *katori*	Namkeen sprouted dalia - ½ *katori*
3.00 p.m.	Milk - 1 small glass	Milk - 1 small glass
6.00 p.m.	Mashed banana - 1	Stewed fruit - ½ *katori*
8.00 p.m.	Vegetable soup - 1 *katori*	Suji halwa - ¼ *katori*
10.00 p.m.	Milk - 1 small glass	Milk - 1 small glass

Sample Menu for 1 to 2-year-old Child

Time	Monday	Tuesday
Early morning 6.00 a.m.	Milk - 1 glass	Milk - 1 glass
Breakfast 9.00 a.m.	Cheese toast - 1 Apple - one-half	Besan chilla - 1 Guava - one-half
Midmorning 11.30 a.m.	Fruit juice - 1 glass	Melon slices - 2
Lunch 1.30 p.m.	Curd - ½ *katori* Rajma - ½ *katori* Rice - 1 *katori* Salad - a few pieces	Kadhi - ½ *katori* Rice - 1 *katori* Ladies' fingers - ¼ *katori* Salad - a few pieces
Teatime 5.00 p.m.	Fruit milkshake - 1 glass Germinated chaat - ½ *katori*	Bournvita milk - 1 glass Biscuits - 2
Dinner 8.30 p.m.	Paneer-matar - ½ *katori* Spinach parantha - 1	Egg curry - ½ *katori* Paneer parantha - 1
10.00 p.m.	Milk if required, or dessert	

Sample Menu for 4 to 5-year-old Child

Time	Monday	Tuesday
Breakfast 8.30 a.m.	Milk - 1 glass Paneer parantha - 1	Milk - 1 glass Beans-on-toast - 1
Midmorning 11.00 a.m.	Fruit chat - ½ bowl	Channa murmura - 1 *katori*
Lunch 1.30 a.m.	Sambhar - ½ *katori* Idli - 1 Fruit custard - 1 *katori*	Raita - ½ *katori* Masoor dal - ½ *katori* Rice - 1½ *katori* Capsicum rings - 2
Teatime 5.00 p.m.	Lassi - 1 glass Sandwich - 1	Mango milk shake - 1 glass Poha - 1 *katori*
Dinner 8.30 p.m.	Vegetable soup - 1 bowl Noodles with tofu - ½ plate Rainbow Sundae - 1 helping	Alu matar - ½ *katori* Chapatti - 2 (small) Salad - a few pieces Carrot halwa - ¼ *katori*

Special Recipes for the Baby

If you want an honest child, be an honest parent.

Drinks

Fruit Cocktail

Ingredients

Grapes	–	250 gm
Pineapple	–	250 gm
Orange	–	500 gm
Apple	–	250 gm
Honey	–	2 tablespoons
Salt	–	½ teaspoon
Black pepper	–	A pinch

Method

1. Squeeze the juice from the oranges.
2. Wash and peel the apples and pineapple.
3. Put the grapes and one cup of water in a blender. Mix twice and strain.

4. Extract juice of apple and pineapple using a non-citrus juicer.
5. Mix all the juices. Add honey, salt and pepper before serving.

   Serving size – 4 glasses.

- This is a vitamin-packed fruit juice cocktail that children cannot resist.

Fruit Delight

Ingredients

Coconut milk	–	125 ml (half glass)
Apple pieces	–	100 gm (1 big)
Green grapes	–	50 gm
Fresh apple juice	–	250 ml (1 glass)
Honey	–	1 tablespoon

Method

1. Blend apple juice with coconut milk.
2. Chop apple into small pieces.
3. Put the juice in a tall glass. Add apple pieces and grapes and serve.

   Serving size – 4 glasses.

- Children like to fish out grapes and apple pieces with a long spoon.

Vegetable Juice

Ingredients

Carrots	–	250 gm (4)
Tomatoes	–	100 gm (2)
Beetroot (chukandar)	–	50 gm (1)
Lemon	–	1 no.
Salt	–	½ teaspoon
Kala namak (black salt)	–	¼ teaspoon
Roasted jeera	–	¼ teaspoon

Method

1. Wash and peel the vegetables.
2. Extract juice in a non-citrus juicer. Strain well.
3. Add lemon juice, salt, kala namak and jeera.
4. Serve cold.

Serving size - 2 glasses.

- Very nutritious and ideal in winters when juicy, red carrots are available in the market.

Mango Milkshake

Ingredients

Milk	–	500 ml (2 glasses)
Mango	–	100 gm (1)
Sugar	–	6 teaspoons
Vanilla essence	–	½ teaspoon
Cinnamon powder	–	A pinch

Method

1. Peel and chop the mango into small pieces.
2. Put cold milk, mango, sugar, vanilla essence, and cinnamon powder in a blender and liquidise.
3. Add crushed ice and mix again. Serve cool.

   Serving size - 2 glasses.

- Instead of mango you can use strawberries, chikoo, pineapple or banana. Shakes combine the goodness of milk with fruits.

Soups

Mushroom Soup

Ingredients

Mushroom	–	100 gm (half packet)
Onion	–	60 gm (1)
Garlic flake	–	1 no.
Milk	–	200 ml (1 cup)
Corn flour	–	1 tablespoon
Salt	–	¾ teaspoon
Black pepper	–	1 pinch
Carrot	–	60 gm (1 small)
Peas	–	50 gm (¼ cup)
Butter	–	2 teaspoons

Method

1. Chop mushroom, onion and garlic finely.
2. Sauté these in butter till soft. Add 2 teacups water. Blend in liquidiser.
3. Dissolve corn flour in a little water.
4. Put in a pan; add milk, spices and bring to boil.
5. Add corn flour mixture, stirring continuously.
6. Add finely chopped carrot and peas and bring to boil again.

   Serving size – 4 small bowls.

- Peas and carrot impart the soup a colourful look. They should be crunchy and not soft.

Sweet Corn Soup

Ingredients

Tender corncobs	–	2
Corn flour	–	1 tablespoon
Capsicum	–	20 gm (½ piece)
Yellow carrot	–	50 gm (1)
MSG (Ajinomoto) powder	–	1/6 teaspoon
Salt	–	¾ teaspoon
Sugar	–	2 teaspoons

Method

1. Carefully, wash and grate the corn on the cob.
2. Put the corn in a cooker, add four teacups of water, salt and sugar and pressure-cook for 10–15 minutes.
3. Cool and blend in a liquidiser.
4. Make a paste of corn flour and water.
5. Put to boil, add MSG; add corn flour paste, stirring continuously.
6. Chop carrot and capsicum very finely.
7. Add to soup and bring to boil.

- Serve with chilly sauce and soya sauce, if required.

Chicken Stock

Ingredients

Chicken breasts	–	2
Onion	–	60 gm (1 medium)
Ginger	–	10 gm (a small piece)
Garlic	–	1 flake
Salt	–	1 teaspoon

Method

1. Put all the ingredients in a pressure cooker along with six cups of water. Cook for 15–20 minutes after the whistle.
2. Cool and strain the stock through a strainer to get clear stock.
3. Discard residue and shred the meat from chicken pieces for further use.

   Serving size – 6 bowls.

- This soup stock is light and nutritious. Recommended for children who suffer from diarrhoea.

Cream of Chicken Soup

Ingredients

Chicken stock	–	1 recipe
Chicken	–	¼ cup (shredded)
Milk	–	1 cup
Butter	–	1 teaspoon
Maida	–	1 teaspoon
Salt	–	¾ teaspoon
Black pepper	–	A pinch

Method

1. Heat butter in pan. Add maida and sauté on low heat for 2 minutes.
2. Add milk, stirring continuously till it boils.
3. Add stock and cook till the soup thickens.
4. Add shredded chicken, salt and pepper.
5. Cook for 5 minutes.

- This rich, creamy soup is ideal for children.

Raitas

Pineapple Raita

Ingredients

Curd	–	500 gm (2½ cups)
Pineapple slices	–	4
Honey	–	2 teaspoons
Cardamom powder	–	½ teaspoon
Raisins (kismis)	–	2 teaspoons
Salt	–	½ teaspoon

Method

1. Chop pineapple slices into small pieces.
2. Beat the curd till it is nice and smooth. Add honey.
3. Add pineapple pieces and salt.
4. Garnish with raisins and serve cold.

   Serving size – 1 bowl.

- Fresh pineapple can be used instead of pineapple slices. Chop fresh pineapple into pieces, add two tablespoons of sugar and one cup of water and pressure-cook for 15 minutes. Cool and use.

Kachumar Raita

Ingredients

Curd	–	500 gm (2½ cups)
Onion	–	60 gm (1 medium)
Cucumber	–	75 gm (1 medium)
Tomato	–	50 gm (1 medium)
Capsicum	–	30 gm (1)
Boiled potato	–	60 gm (1 medium)
Green coriander	–	A few leaves

Salt	–	½ teaspoon
Black salt	–	¼ teaspoon
Roasted ground jeera	–	½ teaspoon

Method

1. Chop onion, tomato, cucumber, capsicum and boiled potatoes into fine cubes.
2. Beat the curd till it is nice and smooth.
3. Add all the vegetables and spices. Serve cold.

   Serving size – 1 bowl.

Salads

Cucumber Boats

Ingredients

Cucumbers	–	2 (medium)
Cabbage	–	4 small leaves
Apple	–	80 gm (1 medium)
Banana	–	100 gm (1 normal size)
Pear	–	75 gm (1 medium)
Grapes	–	20
Pineapple	–	2 slices
Pomegranate (anar)	–	One-half
Lemon	–	1
Salt	–	½ teaspoon
Black pepper	–	A pinch
Sugar	–	1 teaspoon

Method

1. Wash, peel and cut each cucumber longitudinally into two halves.
2. Scoop out the centre of the cucumber pieces carefully.
3. Wash, peel and chop apple, banana, pear and pineapple. Add grapes and anar seeds to it.
4. Then add salt, sugar, black pepper and lemon juice. Mix well.
5. Fill the cucumber boats with the fruits.
6. Pierce a toothpick in the middle of each boat.
7. Attach a cabbage leaf to it forming the sail.

   Serving size – 4 pieces.

- It is a fancy way of serving fruit chat. Children love variations in shape. Alternatively, cut flowers from small melons and place fruit in them.

Sprout Salad

Ingredients

Moong sprouts	–	100 gm (½ cup)
Alfa sprouts	–	25 gm (1/6 cup)
Black gram sprouts	–	100 gm (½ cup)
Paneer	–	50 gm (2 big pieces)
Boiled potato	–	50 gm (1)
Cucumber	–	50 gm (1)
Onion	–	50 gm (1)
Tomato	–	50 gm (1)
Pomegranate seeds	–	50 gm (¼ cup)
Coriander	–	A few leaves
Salt	–	½-¾ teaspoon
Lemon	–	1

Method

1. Steam the kala channa and moong sprouts for 2–3 minutes.
2. Dice paneer, potato, cucumber, tomato, and onion into small pieces.
3. Wash and chop coriander leaves finely and clean pomegranate.
4. Mix all the ingredients together. Add salt and lemon.

   Serving size – 1 plateful.

- Sprouts are rich sources of proteins, B-complex and vitamin C. Variations can be made in the chat by adding grapes, wheat sprouts, green chillies or bhujiya (sev).

Corn Salad

Ingredients

Soft bhutta	–	2
Boiled potato	–	50 gm (1)

Onion	–	50 gm (1)
Tomato	–	50 gm (1)
Cucumber	–	50 gm (1)
Bhujiya (sev)	–	50 gm
Salt	–	½ teaspoon
Lemon	–	1

Method

1. Boil the bhutta in a pressure cooker with salt for 10–15 minutes. Remove the seeds when cool.
2. Chop the onion, tomato, potato, cucumber and coriander leaves finely.
3. Crush the corn seeds lightly in a blender.
4. Add the vegetables, salt and lemon to corn.
5. Top with sev and serve.

   Serving size – 1 bowl.

- The corn is crushed lightly so that the child does not choke on it.

Coleslaw

Ingredients

Cabbage	–	200 gm (1 small)
Apple	–	100 gm (1 big)
Orange	–	100 gm (1 big)
Celery	–	A few sticks

Dressing

Salad oil	–	1 tablespoon
Cream	–	1 tablespoon
Mustard powder	–	A pinch
Castor sugar	–	2 teaspoons
Salt	–	¼ teaspoon
Lemon	–	1 (extract juice)
Black pepper	–	A pinch

Method

1. Chop cabbage finely and keep in ice-cold water for 15 minutes.
2. Cut the apple into cubes. Peel the orange slices.
3. Chop the celery.
4. Mix all the dressing ingredients together.
5. Mix the dressing with the cabbage, apple, orange and celery. Serve cold.

   Serving size – 1 bowl.

- You can use carrots, pineapple and grapes in the salad. This salad is rich in vitamins A, C and iron.

Macaroni–Peas Salad

Ingredients

Shell macaroni (boiled)	–	200 gm (1 cup)
Peas shelled (boiled)	–	200 gm (1 cup)
Carrot	–	150 gm (2 big)
Cucumber	–	75 gm (1 medium)
Pineapple	–	2 slices (diced)

Dressing

Curd	–	100 gm (½ cup)
Mustard powder	–	A pinch
Honey	–	1 teaspoon
Tomato sauce	–	1 tablespoon
Salt	–	½ teaspoon
Black pepper	–	A pinch

Method

1. Drain the curd for one hour in a muslin cloth.
2. Mix all the dressing ingredients together and cool.
3. Wash, peel and dice carrots and cucumbers.
4. Mix macaroni, peas, carrots, cucumber and pineapple. Add the dressing. Chill and serve.

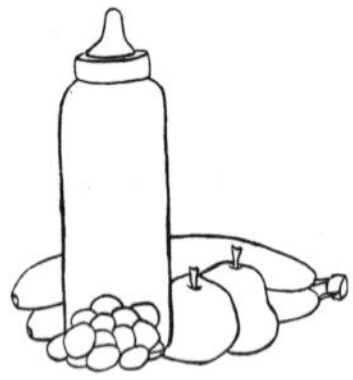

Paneer Wrap

Ingredients

Atta	–	25 gm (2 tablespoons)
Besan	–	15 gm (1 tablespoon)
Paneer	–	50 gm (2 big pieces)
Onion	–	50 gm (1)
Tomato sauce	–	2 teaspoons
Oil	–	1 teaspoon
Cumin seeds	–	¼ teaspoon
Coriander	–	A few leaves

Method

1. Make atta and besan dough.
2. Put oil in a pan and roast the cumin seeds in it.
3. Chop the onion finely and fry in oil.
4. Make small cubes of paneer and add to the onion.
5. Add tomato sauce and chopped coriander leaves.
6. Make two small thin chapattis out of the dough.
7. Put a little filling and roll the chapatti into a pipe-like form.
8. Roll this in an aluminium foil and seal it at one end.
9. Teach the child how to eat the wrap after removing little bits of the foil.

   Serving size – 2 wraps.

- A variety of fillings made from potato, peas, capsicum, carrot etc. can be put into the wrap. This is a complete meal in itself, which contains foods from all the food groups.

Moong Dal Chilla Rolls

Ingredients

Moong dal dhuli	-	50 gm (1/3 cup)
Coriander leaves	-	A few
Oil	-	2 teaspoons
Cucumber	-	50 gm (half)
Paneer	-	50 gm (2 big pieces)
Tomato	-	50 gm (1)
Salt	-	½ teaspoon

Method

1. Soak dal for 3–4 hours and then grind to a fine paste.
2. Add chopped coriander leaves and salt to the paste.
3. Pour a tablespoonful of mixture on a non-stick pan (tava) and spread to get a thin circle.
4. Use a bit of oil and roast the chilla on both sides.
5. Cut thin slices of cucumber, paneer and tomato.
6. Take a chilla, place one slice each of cucumber, paneer and tomato on it and make a roll.
7. Serve the rolls with mint-coriander chutney.

   Serving size - 6 small rolls.

- If in a hurry, moong dal can be substituted with besan batter (as for pakoras). Make small chillas so that the child can easily handle them.

Noodles with Tofu

Ingredients

Noodles	-	100 gm
Tofu (soya paneer)	-	50 gm
Onion	-	75 gm (1 big)
Capsicum	-	25 gm (small pieces)
French beans	-	25 gm (5)

Carrot	–	50 gm (1 medium)
Peas (tender)	–	50 gm (10 pods)
Cabbage	–	50 gm (small piece)
Oil	–	4 teaspoons
Tomato sauce	–	1 tablespoon
Soya sauce	–	2 teaspoons
Vinegar	–	2 teaspoons
Chilli sauce	–	1 teaspoon (optional)
MSG powder	–	½ teaspoon
Salt	–	1 teaspoon

Method

1. Boil water with 1 teaspoon oil in a container. Add noodles, cook till tender and drain water. Wash noodles in cold water and drain well.
2. Chop tofu into small cubes, add oil to pan and sauté tofu for 4–5 minutes.
3. Chop onion, capsicum, carrots, cabbage and French beans into long shreds. Add peas and sauté at high heat for 4–5 minutes.
4. Take 1 teaspoon of oil in a deep pan (*kadai*). Add MSG and vegetables. Stir. Add all the sauces and noodles, and then stir.

   Serving size – 1 bowl.

- Noodles are popular with children. The nutritional content of noodles is enhanced by the addition of tofu and lots of vegetables. Tofu is available at all health food stores.

Macaroni Maaza

Ingredients

Macaroni	–	100 gm (½ packet)
Baby corn	–	100 gm (10 cobs)
Rajma boiled	–	100 gm (½ cup)
Capsicum	–	25 gm (one)
Onion	–	60 gm (1 big)
Cabbage	–	50 gm (small piece)
Tomato sauce	–	2 tablespoons
Chilly sauce	–	1 teaspoon (optional)
Soya sauce	–	1 teaspoon
Salt	–	1 teaspoon
Oil	–	1 tablespoon

Method

1. Boil a big pan of water with ½ teaspoon salt and ½ teaspoon oil.
2. Add macaroni and boil till done. Stir so that macaroni does not stick to the bottom.
3. Drain on a sieve and wash with cold water.
4. Chop baby corn into 2-cm pieces.
5. Chop onion, capsicum and cabbage into 1-cm squares.
6. Add oil to pan and sauté onion, capsicum, corncobs and cabbage on high flame for 5 minutes. Add salt.
7. Add cooked macaroni, rajma and all sauces. Mix well.

   Serving size – 1 bowl.

- A variety of foodstuffs go well with macaroni, e.g. peas, carrot, lobia, paneer.

Pao Bhaji

Ingredients

Potato	–	80 gm (1 big)
Peas	–	100 gm (½ *katori*)
Carrot	–	50 gm (¼ *katori*)
French beans	–	50 gm (¼ *katori*)
Cauliflower	–	50 gm (¼ *katori*)
Capsicum	–	30 gm (1)
Cabbage	–	50 gm (¼ *katori*)
Bottle gourd (ghiya)	–	50 gm (¼ *katori*)
Pumpkin	–	50 gm (¼ *katori*)
Tomato	–	100 gm (2 medium)
Onion	–	100 gm (2 medium)
Ginger-garlic paste	–	1 teaspoon
Salt	–	1 teaspoon
Pao bhaji masala	–	1 teaspoon
Coriander	–	A few leaves
Lemon	–	1
Butter	–	3 teaspoons
Pao buns	–	4

Method

1. Chop all the vegetables, except onion and tomatoes, into small pieces and cook in a pressure cooker till very soft.
2. Put a teaspoon of butter and sauté ginger-garlic paste in a pan for 3–5 minutes.
3. Chop onion and tomato finely and sauté in butter till well cooked.
4. Add all the vegetables, salt, pao bhaji masala and mix very well.
5. At the time of serving put lemon juice, coriander leaves and small butter cubes on top.

6. Cut each pao bun into two. Butter toast on tava and serve alongside bhaji.

   Serving size: For two children.

- Pao bhaji is a good vegetable dish for finicky vegetable eaters. Watch children as they finish their bhaji and ask for more. Any seasonal vegetables can be put in the bhaji.

Club Sandwich

Ingredients

Big bread slices	–	6
Butter	–	20 gm
Cheese	–	2 slices
Tomato	–	100 gm (2 medium)
Cucumber	–	75 gm (1 normal size)
Lettuce	–	25 gm (4 leaves)
Capsicum	–	25 gm (half)
Salt	–	½ teaspoon
Black pepper	–	A pinch
Coriander	–	A few leaves

Method

1. Cut thin slices of tomato, cucumber and capsicum.
2. Chop coriander leaves finely and cut lettuce leaves the size of a bread slice.
3. Toast the bread slices in a toaster and apply butter.
4. Take a toast and spread a lettuce leaf on it. Put a layer of tomatoes. Sprinkle salt, pepper and green coriander on it. Cover it with a second toast.
5. Take one more toast and put a cheese slice, a cucumber layer and a thin layer of capsicum. Cover this with another toast.
6. Cut the toasts diagonally. You will obtain 4 triangular club sandwiches.

7. For comfortable eating, wrap each sandwich partially with a tissue paper.
8. Serve with tomato sauce.

   Serving size: 6 pieces.

- This sandwich can be toasted in a waffle iron too. Instead of cheese, you can also use paneer.

Disco Idli

Ingredients

Suji	–	200 gm (1 cup)
Sour curd	–	75 gm (3/4 cup)
Carrot	–	50 gm (1 medium)
Cabbage	–	50 gm (small piece)
Capsicum	–	25 gm (half)
Salt	–	1 teaspoon
Oil	–	1 teaspoon
Eco	–	1 pouch

Method

1. Sieve suji, then add sour curd and salt to it. Mix well and keep for 20 minutes.
2. Wash, peel and cut carrot, cabbage and capsicum into very fine pieces. Mix with suji.
3. Grease a disco idli mould (for 2-cm diameter idlis).
4. Put 1½ teacup of water in a pressure cooker and heat.
5. Mix the eco in the batter. Spoon the mixture into the disco idli mould and place in the cooker for steaming.
6. Close the lid of the pressure cooker. Steam idlis for 5–7 minutes.
7. Allow to cool and then remove from the mould.
8. Serve with coconut chutney.

   Serving size: 2 plates.

- Do not keep the weight (whistle) on the pressure cooker. In another variation, you can add cashew nuts, almonds and chironji, instead of vegetables.

Quick Colourful Uthapam

Ingredients

Suji	–	100 gm (1 *katori*)
Curd	–	50 gm (½ cup)
Onion	–	50 gm (1 medium)
Tomato	–	50 gm (1 medium)
Capsicum	–	25 gm (half)
Cabbage	–	25 gm (small piece)
Coriander	–	A few leaves
Salt	–	½ teaspoon
Oil	–	20 gm (4 teaspoons)
Til	–	1 teaspoon

Method

1. Mix suji, curd and water to make a thick batter. Keep aside for an hour.
2. Chop onion, tomato, capsicum, cabbage and coriander finely.
3. Put a ladleful of suji mixture on a non-stick pan.
4. Sprinkle the vegetable mixture evenly and put a pinch of til on top.
5. Apply oil on the sides of the uthapam.
6. Turn and cook on the other side.
7. Serve with coconut chutney.

   Serving size: 3–4 small uthapams.

- The urad dal and rice batter used for making dosas is normally used for making uthapams. This is a nourishing main meal or snack for the child.

Germinated Channa Tikkies

Ingredients

Germinated black gram	–	100 gm (1 *katori*)
Boiled potatoes	–	125 gm (2 big)
Rice flakes	–	50 gm (½ *katori*)
Green chilli	–	1 (optional)
Salt	–	½ teaspoon
Amchur	–	½ teaspoon
Oil	–	30 gm

Method

1. Steam the black gram for 5 minutes in a pressure cooker and then crush in a blender.
2. Peel and grate boiled potatoes.
3. Soak the rice flakes for 10 minutes and then drain off excess water.
4. Chop the green chilli very finely.
5. Mix black gram, potatoes, rice flakes, green chilli and add salt and amchur.
6. Make 6 round tikkies.
7. Shallow fry on tava with oil till golden brown.

   Serving size: 6 tikkies.

- Germinated black gram and rice flakes are good sources of iron. Curd can be added on top, before serving.

Mixed Fritters

Ingredients

Potato	–	80 gm (1 big)
Onion	–	100 gm (2 medium)
Cauliflower	–	100 gm (7–8 florets)

Peas shelled	–	100 gm (12–15 pods)
Spinach	–	50 gm (10 leaves)
Cabbage	–	50 gm (small piece)
Green chilli	–	1 (optional)
Salt	–	1 teaspoon
Besan	–	100 gm (1 *katori*)
Ajwain	–	½ teaspoon
Oil for frying		

Method

1. Clean and chop all vegetables into 1-cm pieces.
2. Chop green chilli finely.
3. Mix diced potato, cauliflower, shelled peas, onion, spinach and cabbage.
4. Make thick batter of besan with water. Add salt and ajwain.
5. Mix all the vegetables in the batter.
6. Deep fry small pakoras in oil.
7. Serve with sauce or coriander-mint chutney.

   Serving size: 1 big plateful.

- Any seasonal vegetables like methi, pumpkin etc. can be added to the batter. Take care to deep fry on slow flame or the vegetables may remain raw.

Cheese Toast

Ingredients

Bread slices	–	6
Eggs	–	2
Cheese	–	50 gm (2 cubes)
Maida	–	1 teaspoon
Baking powder	–	A pinch
Mustard powder	–	A pinch
Salt	–	¼ teaspoon

Method

1. Grate the cheese finely.
2. Beat the cheese and egg together with a fork till creamy.
3. Add maida, baking powder, mustard powder and salt and blend well.
4. Spread thickly on one side of bread.
5. Fry to golden-brown colour or bake in preheated oven for 7–10 minutes.

   Serving size: 6 toasts.

- Eggs and cheese are good sources of proteins. Cheese toast can be given at breakfast or teatime.

Baked Beans on Toast

Ingredients

Bread slices	–	4
Rajma	–	100 gm (1 *katori*)
Onion	–	60 gm (1 medium)
Tomato	–	75 gm (2 small)
Ginger	–	A small piece
Jaggery (gur)	–	A small piece
Salt	–	½ teaspoon
Butter	–	2 teaspoons

Method

1. Soak the rajma overnight.
2. Chop onion, tomato and grate ginger.
3. Put onion, tomato, ginger, salt, and jaggery in a pressure cooker along with some water and cook for about 45 minutes. Add only so much water as can be absorbed by the beans. (The beans should be soft.)
4. Toast the bread slices in a toaster and butter them well.
5. Serve beans hot on the toast.

   Serving size: 4 toasts.

- This is an ideal breakfast dish for vegetarians. Each bread slice can be cut into four small pieces for ease in eating.

Channa Jor Garam

Ingredients

Murmura	-	100 gm (2 cups)
Roasted channa	-	50 gm (½ cup)
Roasted cornflakes	-	50 gm (½ cup)
Roasted peanuts	-	50 gm (½ cup)
Oil	-	5 gm (1 teaspoon)
Curry leaves	-	7–8 pieces
Mustard seeds	-	½ teaspoon
Salt	-	½ teaspoon
Turmeric	-	¼ teaspoon

Method

1. Check murmura, channa, cornflakes and peanuts for any impurities or husk.
2. Add oil in the *kadai* and heat. Add mustard seeds and heat till they sputter. Add chopped curry leaves.
3. Add murmura, channa, cornflakes, peanuts, spices and sauté for 4–5 minutes.
4. Cool and store in an airtight tin.

   Serving size: 1 bowl.

- Murmura, channa, peanut and cornflakes are easily available at local shops. This homemade mixture will provide the child with ample calories, proteins and vitamins. This can be turned into a bhelpuri by adding finely chopped onions, coriander leaves and lemon.

Golden Corn on Cob

Ingredients

Soft bhutta	–	2
Salt	–	½ teaspoon
Turmeric	–	A pinch
Sugar	–	1 teaspoon

For Sauce

Tomato sauce	–	2 teaspoons
Amchur	–	½ teaspoon
Salt	–	¼ teaspoon
Black pepper	–	A pinch

Method

1. Peel and wash the corn on cob.
2. Put corn, salt, turmeric and sugar in a pressure cooker. Add ½ cup water.
3. Pressure-cook for 5–10 minutes after the whistle.
4. Put all the ingredients of the sauce in a pan along with 2 teaspoons water. Cook for 2 minutes.
5. Take a whole corncob, pour sauce over it and serve.

   Serving size: 2 bhuttas.

- Children love to take bites of corncob. Corn is nutritious and tasty.

Stuffed Potatoes

Ingredients

Potatoes	–	200 gm (3 big)
Malai	–	2 teaspoons
Cheese	–	2 teaspoons
Onion	–	50 gm (1 medium)
Capsicum	–	20 gm (half)

Salt	–	1/6 teaspoon
Black pepper	–	A pinch

Method

1. Boil the potatoes, but do not remove jackets. Cut them into two halves.
2. Scoop out potato from the middle leaving a wall of half centimetre.
3. Mix malai and scooped-out potato.
4. Cut onion and capsicum finely.
5. Mix with potato and malai mixture. Add salt and pepper.
6. Refill potatoes with the potato mixture.
7. Bake at 250°C till golden brown.

   Serving size: 1 plate.

- Paneer and pea filling can also be used.

Crunchy Kebabs

Ingredients

Boiled potatoes	–	175 gm (3 big)
Boiled peas	–	75 gm (½ *katori*)
Cabbage	–	25 gm (small piece)
Capsicum	–	25 gm (one)
Green chilli	–	1 (optional)
Roasted peanuts	–	50 gm (¼ *katori*)
Besan	–	50 gm (½ *katori*)
Til	–	25 gm (1/6 *katori*)
Salt	–	1 teaspoon
Amchur	–	½ teaspoon
Garam masala	–	¼ teaspoon
Coriander	–	A few leaves
Oil for frying		

Method

1. Chop cabbage, capsicum and green chilli finely.
2. Mash boiled potatoes and add peas, vegetables, roasted peanut and spices.
3. Mix besan and water to make a thin batter.
4. Shape the potato mixture into small rod-shaped bits.
5. Dip each kebab in besan and then roll in til.
6. Deep fry till golden brown.
7. Serve with tomato sauce or coriander chutney.

   Serving size: 1 plate.

- Any seasonal vegetables like French beans, carrots, etc. can be steamed and put in the mixture.

Spinach Squares Chaat

Ingredients

Refined flour (maida)	–	100 gm (3/4 *katori*)
Ground spinach	–	50 gm (1/4 *katori*)
Boiled potato	–	50 gm (1medium)
Boiled channa	–	50 gm (1/4 *katori*)
Curd	–	100 gm (1 *katori*)
Salt	–	1/2 teaspoon
Jeera	–	1/4 teaspoon
Ajwain	–	A pinch
Quick saunth	–	1 tablespoon
Oil	–	1 tablespoon
Oil for frying		

Method

1. Sift maida, add a pinch of ajwain and 1/4 teaspoon salt.
2. Wash and grind spinach leaves to give 1/4 *katori* thick spinach puree.
3. Add spinach puree to maida along with a teaspoon of oil. Add enough water to make smooth hard dough.

4. Divide the dough into four parts.
5. Roll out each ball into a flat thin chapatti.
6. With a sharp knife cut out 2-cm squares.
7. Cut out squares from all the dough.
8. Deep fry squares till golden brown.
9. Set a few squares on a plate and top with boiled channa and cubed boiled potato. Spread curd, salt and saunth on top. Garnish with roasted ground jeera and red chillies (optional).

   Serving size: 2 plates.

- Spinach squares can be eaten as they are with pickle, sauce or coriander chutney. They can be stored for a week in an airtight box.

Quick Saunth

Amchur powder	–	1 tablespoon
Sugar	–	2 tablespoons
Salt	–	½ teaspoon
Kala namak	–	1/6 teaspoon
Jeera (roasted)	–	1/6 teaspoon
Garam masala	–	1/6 teaspoon
Water	–	2 tablespoons
Red chillies	–	1/6 teaspoon (optional)

Method

Mix all the ingredients well in a thick-bottomed pan. Keep on fire and cook till a smooth, thick, sauce is obtained.

Matar–Mushroom in Cream

Ingredients

Mushrooms	–	200 gm (1 small packet)
Peas (shelled)	–	200 gm (2 cups)
Tomato	–	120 gm (2 medium)
Cream or malai	–	½ *katori*
Ginger	–	A small piece
Green chilli	–	1
Jeera	–	1 teaspoon
Salt	–	1 teaspoon
Dhania powder	–	1 teaspoon
Garam masala	–	¼ teaspoon
Oil	–	1 tablespoon
Coriander	–	A few leaves

Method

1. Blanch peas in salted water for 5 minutes.
2. Grind ginger, green chilli and tomatoes in blender.
3. Take oil in a pan and heat jeera.
4. Add tomato puree, salt, dhania powder and cook till almost dry.
5. Cut mushrooms into longitudinal slices.
6. Sauté in tomato paste for 3–4 minutes.
7. Add blanched peas and cream. Cook for 3–4 minutes.
8. Garnish with coriander leaves.

   Serving size: 1 bowl.

- These are mild yet interestingly flavoured mushrooms. Pieces of cashew nuts can be added to the dish, if the children like it that way.

Stir–fried Vegetables

Ingredients

Cabbage	–	100 gm (½ small-sized)
Carrot	–	125 gm (2 medium)
Capsicum	–	50 gm (two)
Onion	–	50 gm (1 medium)
Cauliflower	–	100 gm (a few florets)
French beans	–	100 gm (ten)
Salt	–	1 teaspoon
Refined oil	–	1 tablespoon
Black pepper	–	A pinch

Method

1. Cut carrots, French beans, capsicum, onion and cabbage into matchstick-sized pieces.
2. Break cauliflower into small florets.
3. Take oil in a *kadai* and add all the vegetables.
4. Add salt and black pepper and sauté for 5–10 minutes on high flame, stirring continuously.
5. Add a dash of chilli and soya sauce if required.

   Serving size: 1 bowl.

- Vegetables should be crisp. Prepare just before serving.

Crisp Cabbage with Coconut

Ingredients

Cabbage	–	500 gm (1 medium)
Green chilli	–	1
Ginger	–	A small piece
Coriander	–	A few leaves
Refined oil	–	1 tablespoon
Salt	–	1 teaspoon

Mustard seeds	–	½ teaspoon
Fresh coconut	–	2 tablespoons

Method

1. Chop green chilli, ginger and cabbage finely.
2. Spread cabbage on a plate, sprinkle salt on and leave for 5 minutes.
3. Put oil in a *kadai* and fry mustard seeds in it.
4. Add green chilli and ginger and sauté for 2 minutes.
5. Add cabbage leaves and sauté for 5 minutes on high flame.
6. Garnish with coriander leaves and fresh coconut.

   Serving size: 1 bowl.

- Make cabbage in this style for a change in taste. The vegetable is crunchy and can also be served as a salad.

Ladies' Fingers with Baby Onions

Ingredients

Ladies' fingers	–	350 gm
Onion	–	100 gm (2 medium)
Green chilli	–	1
Mustard oil	–	1 tablespoon
Salt	–	1 teaspoon
Turmeric	–	¼ teaspoon
Ground saunf	–	1 teaspoon
Coriander powder	–	1 teaspoon
Amchur	–	1 teaspoon
Ajwain	–	¼ teaspoon

Method

1. Wash, dry and cut ladies' fingers into 2-cm pieces.
2. Peel, wash and make two cuts (like a cross) on each onion.

3. Heat mustard oil in *kadai* and add ajwain.
4. Add onions and sauté for 5 minutes.
5. Add ladies' fingers and all other spices except amchur. Cover with lid.
6. Cook on slow fire, stirring occasionally.
7. Remove lid and further sauté for 5 minutes.
8. Add amchur and sauté again till crisp.

Serving size: 1 bowl.

- Ladies' finger is a vegetable relished by children. Make sure it is totally dry before cooking.

Broccoli, Mushroom, Baby Corn in Cream

Ingredients

Broccoli	–	200 gm (1 small flower)
Mushroom	–	100 gm (15 mushrooms)
Baby corn	–	10 cobs
Butter	–	2 teaspoons
Salt	–	½ teaspoon
Black pepper	–	A pinch
Cream or malai	–	2 tablespoons

Method

1. Break the broccoli into small florets.
2. Chop mushrooms.
3. Chop baby corn into 2-cm pieces.
4. Put butter in saucepan and sauté broccoli, mushrooms and baby corn for 5–7 minutes.
5. Add salt, black pepper and cream and sauté again for 4–5 minutes.

Serving size: 1 bowl.

- Broccoli and mushroom taste best when sautéed slightly. Broccoli is rich in antioxidants.

Capsicum Rings

Ingredients

Capsicum	–	100 gm (2 big)
Potatoes (boiled)	–	120 gm (2 big)
Oil	–	1 tablespoon
Salt	–	½ teaspoon
Amchur	–	¼ teaspoon
Garam masala	–	A pinch

Method

1. Chop capsicum into 1-cm-thick rings carefully.
2. Grate the boiled potatoes and put all the spices in it. Mix well.
3. Place a capsicum ring on chopping board and stuff potato filling in it. Treat all capsicum pieces like this. (Capsicum rings should look like flat tikkies.)
4. Place the rings on a tava and add oil. Cook well on both sides till golden brown.

   Serving size: 1 plate.

- Kiddies may not like capsicums, but they will like these capsicum-ring tikkies.

Cereals

Red Roti

Ingredients

Atta	–	50 gm (½ *katori*)
Carrot	–	75 gm (1 medium)
Salt	–	A pinch

Method

1. Wash, peel and grate carrot finely.
2. Add to atta with salt and knead the dough.
3. Divide the dough into two small balls.
4. Roll out roti and roast on tava.

   Serving size: 2 rotis.

Green Parantha

Ingredients

Atta	–	50 gm (½ *katori*)
Spinach	–	50 gm
Salt	–	A pinch
Oil	–	2 teaspoons

Method

1. Clean, chop, boil and grind the spinach.
2. Add to atta. Add salt and knead the dough.
3. Divide the dough into two small balls.
4. Roll out parantha.
5. Roast on tava with a little oil.

   Serving size: 2 paranthas.

Pearl Parantha

Ingredients

Atta	–	50 gm (½ *katori*)
Moong (dhuli)	–	20 gm (4 teaspoons)
Salt	–	1/6 teaspoon
Ajwain	–	A pinch
Oil	–	2 teaspoons

Method

1. Soak dhuli moong dal for 2 hours.
2. Drain and add to atta.
3. Add salt, ajwain and knead the dough.
4. Divide the dough in 2–3 balls.
5. Roll out a parantha.
6. Roast on tava with a little oil.

Nutritious Roti

Ingredients

Atta	–	50 gm (½ *katori*)
Soyabean flour	–	10 gm (2 teaspoons)
Bathua	–	10 gm (a few leaves)
Salt	–	A pinch

Method

1. Wash, clean and chop bathua finely.
2. Mix soyabean flour with atta, adding the bathua and salt.
3. Knead to a soft dough and prepare small balls.
4. Roll out chapattis and roast on tava.

   Serving size: 2 rotis.

Power Parantha

Ingredients

Atta	–	50 gm (½ *katori*)
Besan	–	20 gm (4 teaspoons)
Onion	–	20 gm (1 small)
Chulai (amaranthus)	–	25 gm (a few leaves)
Salt	–	A pinch
Oil	–	10 gm

Method

1. Wash, clean and chop chulai finely.
2. Add besan to atta.
3. Chop onion finely.
4. Add onion, chulai and salt and knead the dough.
5. Roll out chapattis and roast on tava.
6. Apply oil on both sides.

   Serving size: 2 rotis.

- A lot of emphasis has been placed on fortification of chapattis with vegetables, because children get to eat green vegetables in this way. Any seasonal green leafy vegetable like methi, bathua, chulai, kulfa can be added to the chapattis.

Cool Curd Rice

Ingredients

Rice	–	100 gm (1 *katori*)
Curd	–	200 gm (2 *katori*)
Tomato	–	50 gm (1 medium)
Onion	–	50 gm (1 medium)
Cucumber	–	50 gm (1 small)
Mango (green) ambi	–	10 gm
Oil	–	5 gm

Coriander	–	A few leaves
Mustard seeds	–	½ teaspoon
Curry leaves	–	A few
Salt	–	½–¾ teaspoon

Method

1. Boil rice with twice the amount of water.
2. Wash, peel and chop tomato, onion, cucumber, and ambi into fine cubes.
3. Cool the rice and add curd to it.
4. Add chopped vegetables, coriander leaves and salt to the rice and curd mixture.
5. Prepare a baghar of mustard seeds and curry leaves in oil. Add to rice. Mix well.
6. Cool the rice for 3–4 hours in refrigerator.
7. Serve chilled.

   Serving size: 1 bowl.

- Children love this version of curd rice. If the child is fond of fruits, ripe mango and apple pieces can be added to the rice.

Red Rice

Ingredients

Rice	–	100 gm (1 *katori*)
Tomato	–	100 gm (2 medium)
Carrot	–	100 gm (2 medium)
Boiled rajma	–	25 gm (¼ *katori*)
Oil	–	5 gm (1 teaspoon)
Salt	–	½–¾ teaspoon

Method

1. Wash, peel and grate carrots.
2. Wash, chop and blend tomatoes in liquidiser.
3. Boil rice with oil and grated carrots. When they are nearly done, add the tomato puree and rajma.
4. Cook till liquid dries up.

   Serving size: 1 bowl.

Pulses

Panchmale Dal

Ingredients

Channa dal	–	15 gm (1 tablespoon)
Urad chilka	–	15 gm (1 tablespoon)
Green gram (moong chilka)	–	15 gm (1 tablespoon)
Masoor dal	–	15 gm (1 tablespoon)
Arhar dal	–	15 gm (1 tablespoon)
Ginger	–	A small piece
Green chilli	–	1 (optional)
Onion	–	50 gm (1 medium)
Tomato	–	60 gm (1 medium)
Garlic	–	2 flakes
Ghee	–	1 tablespoon
Turmeric powder	–	½ teaspoon
Salt	–	1 teaspoon
Hing	–	A small crystal
Jeera	–	½ teaspoon
Green coriander	–	A few leaves

Method

1. Chop green chilli, ginger, garlic, onion and tomato finely.
2. Wash, clean and soak all dals together for ten minutes.
3. Heat ghee in pressure cooker, adding hing and jeera. Fry for 2 minutes.
4. Add garlic and ginger and fry. Add onions and tomatoes and fry for another 5 minutes.
5. Add dals, four cups of water, salt and turmeric, and cook for 15 minutes.

6. Garnish with coriander.
7. Serve with boiled rice or chapatti.

   Serving size: 1 bowl.

- This combination of five dals is not only tasty but very nutritious too.

Sambhar

Ingredients

Arhar dal	–	100 gm (1 *katori*)
Onion	–	50 gm (1medium)
Cabbage	–	25 gm (a small piece)
Drumsticks	–	2 pieces
Tomato	–	50 gm (1 medium)
Brinjal	–	25 gm (a small piece)
Pumpkin	–	25 gm (a small piece)
Imli (tamarind)	–	50 gm (a 3-cm ball)
Turmeric powder	–	½ teaspoon
Salt	–	1½ teaspoons
Sugar	–	1 teaspoon
Oil	–	1 teaspoon
Mustard seeds	–	1 teaspoon
Methi seeds (curry leaves)	–	A few

Sambhar Powder

Channa dal	–	1 teaspoon
Methi seeds	–	1 teaspoon
Jeera	–	1 teaspoon
Hing	–	A little crystal
Red chilli	–	1
Black pepper	–	A few corns

Method

1. Dry roast all the ingredients of the sambhar powder for 5 minutes. Then grind them.
2. Boil arhar dal with salt and turmeric for about 15 minutes till well done.
3. Chop all vegetables into small pieces.
4. Take ½ tablespoon oil in a *kadai*. Fry vegetables for 5–7 minutes.
5. Soak imli for half an hour and extract tamarind pulp.
6. Add imli, vegetable, sambhar powder and sugar to dal and cook for 5 minutes.
7. Prepare a baghar (chonk) of mustard seeds and curry leaves, then add to sambhar.
8. Serve hot with rice or idlis.

   Serving size: 1 bowl.

- Any seasonal vegetables like radish, ladies' fingers, ghiya or cauliflower can be added to sambhar. Sambhar is an excellent combination of pulses and vegetables. Freshly prepared sambhar powder has a lovely fragrance.

Sindhi Curry

Ingredients

Tamarind pulp	–	3 tablespoons
Besan	–	150 gm (1½ *katori*)
Green chilli	–	1
Ginger	–	A small piece
Mixed vegetables (potato, ladies' fingers, brinjal, lotus stem, peas, carrot, tindas)	–	200 gm (2 *katoris*)
Cumin seeds (jeera)	–	1 teaspoon
Methi seeds	–	½ teaspoon
Hing	–	1 small crystal
Salt	–	1 teaspoon

Curry leaves	–	A few
Oil	–	2 tablespoons

Method

1. Cut potato, ladies' fingers, brinjal, lotus stem, carrot and tindas into big pieces. Stir and fry them in oil for 5 minutes.
2. Put a tablespoon of oil in a cooker. Add hing, curry leaves, methi seeds, and cumin seeds, then fry.
3. Add besan and cook on slow heat, stirring continuously till besan emits a fragrance and is light brown in colour.
4. Add 6 cups of water, salt, green chillies, ginger, tamarind pulp and cook till 2–3 boils are obtained.
5. Add vegetables and cook till tender.

   Serving size: 1 bowl.

- Add any seasonal vegetable to the curry. It is full of nutrients and taste.

Rainbow Sundae

Ingredients

Orange jelly	–	½ packet
Lemon jelly	–	½ packet
Vanilla ice cream	–	2 small cups
Fresh cherries	–	½ *katori*
Pineapple chunks	–	3
Mango	–	100 gm (one)
Apple	–	80 gm (one)
Wafer biscuits	–	3
Cream	–	50 gm (½ *katori*)
Castor sugar	–	2 tablespoons

Method

1. Prepare the jellies according to directions given on the packet.
2. Beat cream with sugar till thick.
3. Cut small cubes of mango, apple and pineapple. Cut cherries into halves and remove pip.
4. Take two tall dessert glasses.
5. Put alternate layers of jelly, fruit, ice cream and cream.
6. Cover top with cream. Put a cherry and wafer biscuit on top.

   Serving size: 2 glasses.

- Children love this combination of fruits, jelly and ice cream. Fruits like grapes, pomegranate, peas, peaches and banana etc. can also be used.

Eggless Almond Cake

Ingredients

Maida	–	1½ cup
Granulated sugar	–	¾ cup
Fresh curd	–	1 cup
Oil	–	½ cup
Almonds	–	50 gm
Baking powder	–	1 teaspoon
Baking soda	–	½ teaspoon
Vanilla essence	–	1 teaspoon

Method

1. Sieve maida, baking powder and baking soda together.
2. Add sugar to curd and beat this till sugar dissolves.
3. Add oil, vanilla essence, and dry ingredients to curd and sugar mixture.
4. Chop almonds finely and put in the mixture. Save some almonds for decoration on top of the mixture.
5. Put mixture into a cake tin. Bake in a preheated oven for 10 minutes at 200°C and 10–15 minutes at 150°C.

   Serving size: 1 medium cake.

- After mixing all ingredients keep immediately for baking for best results. Lots of variations can be made with this basic cake e.g. adding tutti-fruti fruits or chocolate powder and cocoa.

Nutritious Laddu

Ingredients

Atta	–	100 gm (1 *katori*)
Besan	–	100 gm (1 *katori*)
Burra or ground sugar	–	200 gm (2 *katoris*)
Oil or ghee	–	100 gm (1 *katori*)

Til	–	25 gm (5 teaspoons)
Peanuts	–	25 gm (5 teaspoons)

Method

1. Dry roast til and peanuts separately.
2. Grind peanuts coarsely.
3. Add atta and besan to heated oil in a *kadai*.
4. Cook on slow heat till besan and atta turn very light brown and fragrance is emitted.
5. Remove from heat, add sugar, til and peanuts and mix well.
6. Cool and shape into laddus.

   Serving size: 20 small laddus.

- These laddus make an excellent snack and can also be given for school tiffin. Almonds, cashew nuts, raisins and chironji can be added to the laddus.

Paneer Pudding

Ingredients

Milk	–	250 gm (1 glass)
Paneer	–	50 gm (2 big pieces)
Sugar	–	15 gm (3 teaspoons)
Elaichi	–	1
Almonds	–	5 gm
Cherries	–	4

Method

1. Heat milk till it thickens a bit.
2. Add crumbled paneer and cook till milk and paneer blend well.
3. Add crushed elaichi and sugar.
4. Add soaked chopped almonds to it and cool.
5. Cut cherries and use for decoration.

   Serving size: 1 bowl.

- This is a very nutritious pudding, fit for all age groups.

Household Measures Used for Measuring Ingredients

A teaspoon (standard size)	-	5 gm or 5 ml
A tablespoon (standard size)	-	15 gm or 15 ml
A *katori* (standard size)	-	100–120 gm
A teacup (average size)	-	200 ml
A glass (average size)	-	250 ml
A big glass	-	350 ml